On the Vistula Facing East

2/19/00

To Dad,
We hope you
have a healthy and
happy both birthday!
We Love you very
much!!

Love,
Debbie, Charlie, Rachel and Melanie

On the Vistula
Facing East

Frank Meisler

André Deutsch

On the Vistula
Facing East

Frank Meisler

André Deutsch

First published in 1996 by
André Deutsch Limited
106 Great Russell Street
London WC1B 3LJ

CIP data for this title is available
from the British Library

ISBN 0 233 99022 4

Printed in Great Britain

Contents

Acknowledgements

My deep gratitude to Michael Sharp, Lucie Beighton, Vivienne Schuster and Sally Twite for all the help they have given me.

A special 'thank you' to Issy Mindowlife for his patient work on the word processor and good advice throughout.

My apologies to Batya Melcher, Arie Ovadia, Sara Arbel, Elana Closenberg and other colleagues, for the many hours I spent writing this book in preference to other urgent priorities.

While writing this book, I find good cause to recall the story my mother told me, about a bird who saw a little worm crawling on the ground. Days later, the bird encountered the worm again on top of a high tree. 'How did you get so far?' the astonished bird asked, and the worm replied, 'On my belly, brother, inch by inch.'

Acknowledgments

My deep gratitude to Michael Stark, Lucie Feighan, Vivienne Schuster and Sally Twite for all the help they have given me.

A special 'thank you' to Issy Miodownik for his patient work on the word-processor and good advice throughout.

My apologies to Batya Meisler, Arie Ovadia, Sara Arbel, Elana Closenberg and other colleagues, for the many hours spent writing this book, in preference to other urgent priorities.

While writing this book, I had good cause to recall the story my mother told me, about a bird who saw a little worm crawling on the ground. Days later the bird encountered the worm again on top of a high tree. 'How did you get so far?' the astonished bird asked, and the worm replied, 'On my belly, brother, inch by inch.'

On the Vistula eastward facing
a Grenadier his beat is pacing.
See, a maiden, young and pretty,
brings him flowers from the city.

Danzig Marching Song

Remember days long gone by.
Ponder the years of each generation.
Ask your father and let him tell you,
and your grandfather, who will explain it.

Deuteronomy 32.7

Letter to Franz Boss

MY DEAR GRANDFATHER,
You would like the bar in which I sit as I write this letter. I am in an elegant hotel in Miami, fountains splash in the patio and the afternoon is hot. A Latin-American melody comes from no particular direction: *'Ay mi vida, mi amor! Mi corazón!'* The music is lively, but sad, and reminds me of the gypsy orchestra in the cabaret you owned in Zoppot. I remember your birthday party there. They toasted you with champagne: 'Till one hundred and twenty!' The time has come. You were born one hundred and twenty years ago. Happy birthday!

Tomorrow, a sculpture of mine will be unveiled in the vicinity. Between the work, the speeches and the dinners, I have begun a book intended for your great grand-children, my daughters Michal and Marit. In a few years no one will be alive to remember those I describe. The name of the city we lived in has already vanished from the atlases of the world. This seems the right time and place to begin.

A group of Japanese executives has just risen from the table beside me, bowing to each other at various angles of respect. I look at them as you would have looked at the White Russians, the wealthy exotics of your day, in the elegant hotels of Baden-Baden. My mother told me that on arriving at a hotel *en famille*, you produced a large

1

banknote, tore it in half and promised the staff the other half on departure. She said it always worked wonders.

I have a photograph of you in the foyer of an ornate hotel. You hold a silver-tipped swagger-cane and a jug of spa water. My grandmother, Lucie, has you by the arm. She looks splendid in a bird's-nest hat, veil, fur stole and pearls. You are a short, compact man, in a well-cut suit, with cropped hair, heavy eyebrows, sardonic eyes and a smile to match.

Perhaps I should introduce myself. I am one of your two grandsons, the only child of Meta, your second daughter. I inherited your name, eyebrows, crop of hair and who knows what else among the things I do and am. To the family at large, you were the great legend and I wish that I knew more about you. Those who could have told me are all dead, except for a cousin, who remembers you in your large house, in the 'Moat of the Dominicans'. The streets of our town had sober names, like merchant's inventories, commemorating neither great men nor great events. I was born in the 'Town Moat', and like the 'Moat of the Dominicans' it was a solid and fashionable street.

At Los Angeles airport recently, I asked that cousin how such a successful man could have died destitute. She quoted your brother Georg, her father, who said that you trusted your friends too much and lent them money too freely. It's hard to believe that someone who made such a fortune in difficult times would then have been so careless with it. I know that the delayed impact of the Wall Street Crash was connected with it and that you went down together with two substantial banks. Yet I also know that you loved your friends as you loved the good things of life. The good things killed you in the end and it's quite possible that your good friends played their part in your ruin.

Your father Louis dealt in horses and much of his time was spent travelling around the farmyards and markets of Kashubia. Your education went no further than a few years at a Prussian primary school. As you also began as a horse-trader, you must have learned it from Louis. It was a rough business, with all the tricks that make old horses seem young and defective ones appear fit for the races. 'Turpentine birds' was the term for horses painted up to look sprightly; those without hope, bound for the slaughter-house, were 'soup chickens', and I hear that you also described people that way.

You soon rose higher than Louis and his Kashubian circuit with a contract from the German Army for horses, which you bought in Denmark and the Low Countries. They were tall, broad animals, bred to pull heavy wagons loaded with beer barrels or drag German cannons into battle.

Visiting Copenhagen in 1959, I found the restaurant which you frequented. It was near the fish-market and had an old-time elegance, with oil paintings and chandeliers. Persian rugs were draped over the tables. Cigar fumes enveloped the groups of men who ate there and raised their glasses to the business deals at hand. I had also heard of private rooms upstairs, used for discreet dinners with Danish ladies, but found them dismantled to form an assembly hall of gilt and rosewood. All that remained from those days was the painting of a reclining nude, stroking a contented monkey.

I sat there and wondered where your favourite table would have been fifty years ago, and what you talked about with your horse-trading cronies from Danzig. I even asked the manager whether he still had the guest books of 1912–14. 'I have discovered that the Danzig merchants were excellent customers here,' he said some days later. He also showed me your signature, followed by compliments on the eels you supped on.

Before the 1914–18 war you had already prospered and owned a leather business on the Holzmarkt with branches in Langfuhr and Lauenburg. You were married to Lucie Blumenthal from Elbing, one of four sisters. The others were Jenny, mother of Erich and Kurt, 'Tante Doktor' in Lauenburg and Tante Heidchen, who was simple and could only spell her name and the name of God. During the war, though no longer young, you volunteered and were made Quartermaster in the cavalry. Like your brother Georg, you served in Belgium. You both returned with Iron Crosses and fine Flemish oil paintings as souvenirs of the campaign. They adorned your walls. One was so frightening that I refused to go near it, though it hung in the dining-room. In the picture a young man in a drunken sleep, his head on the dining-table, lay between bottles, cards, spilled wine and all the signs of a Dutch debauchery. A skeleton leaned over him, playing a lute with gaily coloured ribbons, and sang out of its skull. I cried in panic each time I saw it. That painting, looted from some home in Flanders, preached abstinence and sobriety. Perhaps you should have heeded that as you dined in its proximity.

I have a photograph of you in uniform, sent home as a 'Field postcard' from the front. You are mounted on Max, the white-speckled horse you rode and brought home after the war. By the time I grew up Max was very old, chewing on his pouch of oats in Arthur Levandovky's stables. My cousin Peter and I made sounds like exploding shells to see how the ancient war horse would respond. To our disappointment he barely raised his ears and continued to chew, as if to let us know that he had heard and survived more impressive sounds in Flanders.

4

Occasionally after a heavy snowfall, we harnessed Max to a
sleigh and crunched up to Bischofsberg, throwing snow-
balls as we drove. The ancient bastions above the city,
covered in white, seemed as if they had just been evacuated by Napoleon's army in its retreat through Danzig
back from the snows of Russia. Max's amble turned into a
canter there and he pulled us behind him, his nostrils
steaming in the icy air. Suddenly he was young again, as if
something about Bischofsberg reminded him of old times.

While you were at the Front, your women folk did all the
patriotic things at home. My mother told me that they
donated their gold jewellery in exchange for iron replicas
and a certificate saying 'I gave gold for iron.' They also
contributed their long hair, avoided using French words,
the language of the enemy, and ate turnips. Flags were
patriotically stuck into a map to mark the victories at the
Front, but while millions of young men died in the mud,
the flags seldom moved.

You survived the war and returned to prosper, recognising postwar needs and economic opportunities. A
cartoon by Georg Grosz illustrates the time: men with
cigars escort bejewelled women in furs past legless beggars
in uniform. A Germany in defeat and bitterness that was to
breed Nazism a decade later. I have a photograph of you
in your carriage with a coachman in livery. You look content then and content also a little later, in an open-topped,
silver-plated Mercedes, the coachman now a chauffeur.
You sent your daughters to exclusive boarding schools in
Hanover and Lausanne. There they learned the French
they had so patriotically avoided during the war, deportment, riding, and how to deal with lesbian advances by
teachers and older pupils. At carnival time you sponsored
a float from which the three 'Boss Beauties' in costume
threw flowers into the streets of Danzig. Ruth, your eldest,

has black hair, olive skin and the deep, dark eyes of Spanish portraits. Meta, my mother, resembles an attractive, apple-cheeked peasant girl. That ingenuous look was deceptive, however, and in retrospect I can reconstruct her lovers from among the circle of family friends. Elschen, the youngest, was even darker than Ruth. The Sephardic roots of the family were very clear in her, and she faded soon as the youngest child never recovered from the crash that brought down your family. I remember her in elegant riding-clothes, holding her horse, in the company of smart young men. She died alone in Los Angeles many years ago.

When the postwar settlement separated Danzig from Germany and it became a Free City again, you were its Argentinian consul. The diplomatic status enabled you to cross the borders of Danzig, Poland and Germany without the inconveniences of a search, and you made full use of that. The leather business now had additional branches in Berlin, Stettin and Warsaw. 'Leather Boss' had become an international brand name and the 'Free City' status of Danzig allowed you to use the port and customs facilities to good advantage.

You acquired other properties in Danzig, in Germany and locations as far away as the Canary Islands. They included amber mines, saw-mills and cinemas. In the nearby seaside town of Zoppot, you owned a cabaret called 'Cockatoo', and houses, in one of which your summers were spent. We vacationed in a nearby villa. I remember the family processions in black-tie and evening gowns to the 'Waldoper', the Wagnerian operas performed in the forest. But I also saw you one evening at the 'Cockatoo' with a black dancer on your knee, and you gave me five gulden to disappear. It was a small fortune. Many other members of the family were working in what by now has become a commercial empire.

You owned an estate in Pomerania and were on good terms with the neighbouring Prussian landowners, the von Puttkammers and von Butows. You lived your life on many levels: the horse-dealer who knew the language of the gypsies and the nature of the Kashubians; the highly respectable businessman and paterfamilias. On the side, you loved elegant women, village girls, good food, drink and the company of the dubious as well as the respectable. On your estate, you mixed with Prussian junkers and throughout there was that sardonic smile, as though you did one thing but thought another.

For a gala performance of the *Threepenny Opera* in Berlin, my father converted the interior of one of his great trucks into an elegant salon and you drove together to the capital, drinking champagne in good company. On your return, I heard the melody of 'Mack the Knife' for the first time as you whistled it: 'Yes, the shark has mighty teeth and he keeps them in his face, Macky, though, he has a jack-knife and of that there's not a trace.' You and Mack would have understood each other.

As a major benefactor of the Jewish community, you were frequently asked to finance Polish Jews as they passed through Danzig on their way west. 'Give them double,' was your usual reply, 'that way they'll go even further.' They passed through Danzig in tens of thousands, penniless, bound for America. A camp was erected near the Vistula to house them. Soon the American government, alarmed at this migration, imposed restrictions and quotas. Trapped in the camp, the people sat and waited.

Like the other Jewish patricians of Danzig you contributed generously to their maintenance and hurried them on as fast as you could. United in religion, you felt divided from them in all else. America, to you, was a land for the destitute and for failures. Zionism was a hair-brained idea, devised by those *Ostjuden* who preferred sand-dunes to ghettos.

My father, who arrived in Danzig in the early 1920s from Warsaw University, had no intention of moving on. The Treaty of Versailles had made Danzig into a Free Port, through which Poland's foreign trade would have to pass, and he saw the opportunities. At university he had begun as a medical student, but since he fainted every time a corpse was dissected it seemed that he might be better suited to the study of economics. He was soon joined by his younger brother Fimek. The two bachelors set up home together. My father was then in his early twenties and so handsome that when people met me in later life they shrugged in disappointment and whispered, 'How can this be Misha's son?' He was intelligent, debonair and danced a superb tango. An Argentinian violinist and the dance-floor of the Zoppot Casino Hotel where you sat with your daughters one afternoon was the beginning of a romance between my parents. The casino, its white façade facing the sea, was like a lighthouse flashing prosperity and you were on its board of directors.

My father told me how he left the gaming tables there early one morning and noticed a grand piano in the foyer. As a child he had been taught to play the Russian national anthem, 'God protect our Tsar'. He played it now in memory of old times. The sun rose over the Baltic, as he attempted variations in the style of Bach, Wagner and Gershwin. On turning to leave, he was horrified to see half a dozen White Russians, medals on their tuxedos, standing stiffly to attention and quivering with rage. 'I usually lost money there,' my father said, 'but that time I also lost my composure.'

A year later, after that first tango, he asked for your

daughter's hand and you sent detectives to Poland to sweep for flaws. But they found none. Naturally the family, though mostly the men, strongly disapproved of a Pole in their midst. You apparently liked the newcomer and put on a good face, holding a wedding that lasted seven days and had the town on its feet. Then you sent the newlyweds off on their honeymoon to fine hotels in Vienna, Budapest and Istanbul. I was conceived in one of them. Hence I share your taste in good hotels.

Your other son-in-law, Kurt Regensburger (later abbreviated to Regan), was no problem at all. A young doctor from Bavaria, a medical officer in the war, he courted your oldest daughter Ruth after they met in Wiesbaden and took her off to Kissingen, where he became a reputable spa doctor. Ruth, with rows of pearls and a white stole, Kurt in an elegant suit, pose before Zoppot Casino in a photograph I have. They were 'Beautiful People' long before the phrase was coined.

Kurt's younger brother Fritz liked Danzig so well when he came to the wedding that he decided to settle. His chic, bachelor apartment in the 'Lane of the Woolweavers' had a library of art books (the pornographic ones carefully hidden at the rear), which were a great source of inspiration to me. They were limited editions, beautifully bound and typeset on fine textured paper. The lithographs of Casanova's affairs and the adventures of the sex-driven Count Königsmark at the court of the Hanoverians taught me about art and life at the same time. Thus I knew the design of a male chastity belt long before I understood what one did with the object encased in it. More accessible on the bookshelves were the works of Zille, Georg Grosz, Beckmann, Corinth and other German Impressionists. The tomes of Wilhelm Busch, though, were my favourites, for their wicked humour and lunatic preoccupation with detail. My sculptures too seem to contain these qualities. Whether I absorbed them from Busch, I cannot say.

Fritz was a well-dressed man, small and handsome, with broad shoulders, a stylish moustache, warm eyes and a soft Bavarian accent. I took him as a model of the elegant man-about-town; I admired his manicured nails, tailored suits and the whiff of eau de Cologne that was always about him. I liked Fritz, though he was somewhat distant and, like many bachelors, evaded personal engagement. I believe he was one of my mother's lovers and I sensed tensions and undertones there that went above my head. In 1938, Fritz left for the United States where he died, not much later, of a heart attack.

My encounters with you were few and hazy. I remember your amused smile when I was thrown out of synagogue, for assorted misbehaviours, on High Holidays. Beneath the high dome and the great chandelier, you and the other gentlemen, in prayer shawls and top hats, sang, prayed, listened to Rabbi Gruen's sermon and gossiped. My grandmother sat upstairs, half hidden by the balustrade, surrounded by aunts and cousins in splendid hats. My mother, an atheist of principle, stayed away. There was not much for me to do. In my early years I believed that God too was somewhere in the congregation (which, at least theologically speaking, was correct). He was obviously a grown-up and His mood was volatile. He would suddenly demand a great paean of praise, that made the crystals of the chandelier and the tall windows rattle. 'The Lord reigneth; He is robed in majesty!' The fanfares of the organ boomed, the choir soared, Cantor Meisel strained his operatic baritone and the congregation stood on tip-toe. 'The streams have lifted up their mighty waters, breakers of the sea. But more mighty is the Lord on High!' After that God relaxed and gossiped a little with the prominent members of the congregation. Should He emigrate to America? Or Palestine? Even when complete boredom got the better of me and I was thrown out, I thought that He and I would have an understanding in later life. But the Holocaust came and after that we ceased to be on speaking terms.

I recall vomiting over your suit at a Passover meal. 'This boy is totally pissed!' you said, pointing to an empty glass of wine, and you were absolutely right. If I ran into you on the street, I received a pat on the head and a generous tip. You would smoke a cigar and smell of a cologne specially made in your honour: it carried your name, 'Franzbrandwein'. You had a permanent table at the café you frequented. It was usually surrounded by people with requests. A White Russian, who had found a new source of amber, displayed the lumps on a red handkerchief and the map on the round café table. A policeman you had known all your life needed a little help with his daughter's dowry. Your nephews, Erich or Kurt, whichever one of them not laid low by a dose of clap at the time, begged for the key of your *garçonnière* in the 'Lane of the Holy Ghost'.

Your name, after all, had figured on the special currency issued during the great postwar inflation, when a wicker basket was worth more than the trillion Marks it contained. With the other prominent men of Danzig, you underwrote a temporary local currency which stabilised the economy and stimulated trade. You were therefore an address to go to, a man who made things happen.

One day I passed that café and you called me over. You were playing 'skat' with your friends. Pointing to a pile of coins next to your cards you asked, 'what are those?' 'Coins,' I replied. 'How much is it?' you said. I shrugged. 'They're just coins.' You looked at your friends and said: 'This kid will never make a merchant.' I remember that

11

because it angered me. But you were right, I did not become a businessman. In a sense, money has always remained 'just coins' to me, though I have made enough of them by other means.

I know that you had a number of other children in Danzig; some were pointed out to me over the years. 'Whatever was illegitimate in Danzig, if it was human, it was conceived by your grandfather,' a wicked old gentleman told me years later. Your 'official' mistress was Annie Kirsch, mother of my cousin Lottchen. She came from Kiel, and was married to Georg's brother-in-law. Annie was very attractive with fine cheekbones and dark eyes that looked beyond the tobacco shop her husband owned. She was about twenty-six and had been your mistress for some years. This would not have meant anything to me at the time, but I remember the day on which I realised how beautiful she was.

It was Lottchen's birthday party and I was invited. My mother made sure that I looked tidy that day. As we ate our cakes in the apartment above the tobacco shop, a riot broke out in the square below and all the children rushed to the windows. Communists and Nazis were fighting each other. Above the shouting and screams I heard snatches of the *Internationale*, played by a brass band which disintegrated as mounted police galloped in from the side-streets, hitting at the demonstrators with rubber truncheons. It was chaos. The wounded were piled up against the war memorial in the square, from which huge stone warriors with bowed heads looked down on them.

I watched this, standing at Annie's side and gazed with fascination at her profile: the shape of her cheekbones, the line of her nose, her lips parted in excitement at the events below us. The riot in the Wood Market is no doubt recorded as a detail in the political battles for Danzig. To me it was the backdrop to the moment I discovered what it felt like to stand next to a beautiful woman, and I remember that more than I do the riot.

After your death, before the outbreak of war, the Kirsch family emigrated from Danzig to the United States. By then, emigration to America was no longer for the destitute and the failures alone (unless the belief of the Jews of Germany that they were German was in itself the symbol of great failure). On my first visit to New York in 1948 I met Annie again. She took me to her favourite Viennese café in Manhattan. We sat at a pavement table on a warm afternoon and she looked very attractive in the floral summer-dress she wore. Over *Eiskaffee und Schlagsahne* (iced coffee and whipped cream) she explained the difference between the 'white' German Jews of New York and the 'black' Polish ones. I listened to this nonsense with embarrassment, and wondered which part of me was white and which was black, and whether I had the panache to hold her hand and take her to bed. Later in life I learned that, in these matters, to think is to lose. So the moment passed and I never saw her again.

If I did not go to bed with your mistress, I did at least arrange a better resting place for your wife. After you died in Berlin in 1935, Lucie went to live with Ruth and her family. Together they emigrated to London where Kurt became a popular doctor. They were my guardians when I came to England. We did not see each other very often during the time I went to boarding school, the Air Force and university. I last saw Lucie when I stayed with the Regans during a short school holiday and she was very ill. Her stomach had swollen and she cried as she showed it to me through her night-shift. I felt the helplessness of the young when confronted by the tragedy of the old. I mumbled embarrassed words and knew that I was not equal to the occasion. She died suddenly some weeks later and was buried at Hoop Lane Cemetery in Golders Green. Only the few of us who were her family attended the funeral on that damp day. An air-raid siren sounded and distant guns fired into the sky.

She remains in my memory as a kind lady with a charming smile, who's interventions saved me from my mother's wrath when I broke objects or smeared the upholstery with chocolate. Forty years after her death I strolled through Hoop Lane on a carpet of autumn leaves and remembered Lucie. Searching for her grave I found it collapsed, her name almost erased by wind and rain. I erected a new tombstone, adding the names of my parents as a memorial to their deaths in the Holocaust. It gave me my only opportunity to recite *Kaddish*, the prayer for the dead, and to remember my father, saying that that's what sons are for. When my children and I visit, we leave small stones on the grave as tradition demands. It is the sole memorial to my family.

Sometime in the mid-Thirties, I became aware of concerned family conferences and tense conversations which centred on you and your business empire. Serious men with worried faces came and went with files and ledgers. I overheard that you were extremely ill and that your affairs were in a state of collapse. You had already left Danzig for Berlin with Lucie and Elschen. About a year later I was told that you had died. How this empire disintegrated is a mystery and there is no one left to explain it. The malady that killed you is no mystery – it was common enough in those days, when the saying went: 'An hour with Venus, two years with Mercury.' In your case, mercury was no help and the many assignations with the Venuses you loved exacted their price. In Danzig, after you left, I often encountered the echoes of your past. The lady who sold

14

tickets in one of the cinemas you owned regularly smuggled me into the piano pit, where I learned about the Great Life beyond Danzig and dulled my eyesight. When she first recognised me she laughed and said: 'So you are Franz's grandson! You look like him too – a little fighting cock! I bet one day you'll be like him, a proper fighting cock!'

You and your legend faded away, leaving nothing tangible to remember you by. But as there is no elegant exit from life, yours was as good or as tragic as any other. You were a short man who cast a long shadow, but it moved too fast for me to catch up.

The Jewish funeral is a shabby ceremony, meant perhaps to remind us that the time for pretension is past and that decay, personified by unkempt grave-diggers, is waiting. Yet it has its moment of dignity. As the living take leave of the dead, the Rabbi approaches the grave to address the shrouded corpse: 'Forgive us if, during this burial, we have caused you hurt or indignity, for it was not done with ill intent.'

I can only describe you from the little knowledge I acquired, based on family legends and the observations of a small boy. Not enough to take your measure, not enough to know who and what you were. You are my closest male relative – like me, born and raised in Danzig. My father came from far away and the stories he told of his youth were tales from another place, a Chagallian landscape, where a little boy trudges along country roads to a small-town school in the Russia of the Tsar. I feel the loss of knowing so little about you and the fascination of a complex man whom, in part, I must resemble.

There were in the Danzig of your day a number of very respectable German-Jewish entrepreneurs, who lived and died within their role. Who then stood behind the façade of this particular one, Franz Boss, who seemed to be living more than a double life? Is it too simple to expect a single role from a member of a family of Spanish Jews, who, expelled from their home, settled in Holland, changed their name and nationality whenever necessity arose, their location whenever required and always assumed new roles to survive? The sins of the fathers, according to the Bible, are visited upon future generations. But so too are the sins inflicted on the fathers. I believe that this rootlessness was at the core of your being. The outward persona never fitted the nomad within.

For this impudent assumption, for the inevitable omissions and possible hurt, I ask your pardon. In the words of the Jewish funeral liturgy, 'it was not done with ill intent.'

Louis Boss

MY GREAT-GRANDFATHER was Louis Boss. Franz was his eldest son. Louis appeared in my life as a small man with a large nose, who must have shrunk inside the clothes he wore, because his heavy, dark suit and stiff collar were made for someone bigger. A long red handkerchief hung out of his side pocket and he frequently took snuff in a ritual I often saw among Kashubian farmers. A snuff-box of cow's horn was brought out, the men clenched their fists and the donor distributed a little powder into the hollow of thumb and forefinger. The fist went under the nose and the powder disappeared up each nostril, with a sigh that summed up the burden of life. There was a short period of suspended animation during which large, coloured handkerchiefs appeared just in time for a chorus of sneezes and nose wiping. From this practice a permanent brown dewdrop shook precariously under my great-grandfather's nose, causing us all a major problem. Our dilemma on greeting him was to kiss and get out as fast as possible, in the hope that the dewdrop would fall on the head of the next in line. This accounted for a great rush among us, his grandchildren and great-grandchildren, to be first and never, ever, second.

Louis Boss was a Sephardic Jew. The family left Spain in the fifteenth century rather than convert to Catholicism and found refuge in Protestant Holland. In Spain the family name had been Boaz. In Holland they settled in the town of Hertogenbosch, changing their name to Den Bosch (meaning in Dutch a little forest). In his auto-biography, Casanova mentions doing business in nearby Rotterdam with a Sephardic goldsmith called Boaz. It would be nice to think that he was an ancestor, who might have exchanged tips with Casanova about his two major preoccupations: the recipes for seducing women and turn-ing lead into gold.

During the sixteenth century, due to the wars between Holland and Spain which lasted for almost a century, the family blended in with the Portuguese-Jewish community and were registered in their synagogue. It was awkward in Holland at that time to be associated with Spain.

Strong commercial relations existed throughout this period between Holland and Danzig. From a fishing town which supplied the German hinterland with salted herring, Danzig had grown into a major Baltic port, a 'Free City' and a member of the Hanseatic League. Its prosperity came from the export of Polish and Russian timber and grain. Purchased from the feudal estates in the east, vast quantities of logs as well as rafts loaded with grain were floated down the tributaries of the Vistula into the har-bour. From there, merchant ships carried them to Western Europe. The larger merchants in those countries therefore sent their agents, often younger sons of a family business, to supervise the quality and loading of their goods. Much of the merchandise was routed through Amsterdam and Rotterdam, so that there was a strong presence of Dutch factories and agents who worked or had settled in Danzig.

In time this gave the city an unmistakably Dutch char-acter. Rows of merchants' houses stood narrow but high, with forecourts of carved stone against the rising waters, ornamented gables and a crane suspended from each roof to hoist the merchandise. The paintings in homes and civic buildings and the carvings and high altars in the churches, were the work of Dutch and Flemish artists and craftsmen.

Louis' great-grandfather left Holland for Danzig as one such agent, and married and settled there. The first among our family to make an official appearance in Danzig was listed among the militia guarding the city walls during the twenty months' siege of 1807, which ended with the capture of the city by Napoleon. In the following generations the family had become Germanic and I can recall nothing of Sephardic traditions. The custom among Sephardic Jews of passing on the key of their abandoned family home in Spain to the elder son over the generations did not occur with us, as we were descended from a younger branch. What remained was an olive skin, a violent temper – which evaporated as quickly as it came – and a Mediterranean sensuality that made my great-grandfather and grandfather legendary in their day.

Louis Boss' father was called Jaime, the last to have a Spanish name. As that was impossible to pronounce in German, he became known as Heine. In the Franco-Prussian War of the 1870s, Heine simplified the family name to Boss as, in the Francophobia of the time, Den Boss sounded suspiciously French to Prussian ears. Well before the time of Louis Boss, Danzig had lost its international importance, ceased to be a Free City and was a provincial town in the Kingdom of Prussia.

Louis made his living as a horse-trader. Their reputation was similar to that of used car-dealers today and like car-dealers they had ways of making their product look young, sleek and active for just as long as it took to sell it. On completion of each sale, Louis Boss and his Kashubian peasant clients would go through a complex ritual of spitting into their hands and drinking a strong brew called *Machandel* (deal clincher), which sent them reeling on to the next deal. Louis' nose owed as much to this as to his Semitic origins. *Machandel* should not be confused with another liquor called *Danziger Goldwasser* with gold chips floating in it. Danzig was famous for this and, according to my father, it dated back to the time of the rich merchants when there was gold all over the place, some even ending up in bottles. This can still be found in some esoteric duty-free shops and is now made in Polish Danzig. Neither Louis Boss nor his Kashubian farmers would have wasted their time on it.

To exempt him from military service in the Franco-Prussian War, Louis had been married off early by his father. The bride was called Rosa, lived in Karthaus and was seven years his senior. Before her early death she bore him three sons and a daughter. My grandfather, Franz, was the first to arrive. I was told that when he was born, Louis, in the midst of his horse deals and too much *Machandel*, staggered to the Town Hall and registered him as a girl. Prussian bureaucracy did not take kindly to error and it was a long time before that baby girl could officially proceed to become my grandfather. This may well have been the root cause of the legendary number of women he pursued, once he grew up.

By the time I appeared, Louis had mellowed into a respected patriarch, referred to by the family and beyond as *Der Alte Herr* – the old gentleman. His pronouncements, which were short, pithy and wise, delivered in local dialect, were quoted with amused respect and handed on. He spoke the Kashubian language and got on well with the people; 'even the Galuchim,' he used to say, using a mangled Hebrew word for 'Bald Heads' – the priests with shorn pates.

Louis was born on the 3 March 1855, a date I am unable

to forget because on his eightieth birthday, as the youngest member of the family, I was forced to recite a poem composed in his honour. I stood before him in a Tyrolean suit and short leather trousers, complete with a cod-piece, and reeled off the verses:

Mein Lieber Uropapa,
Deine beiden Urenkel sind da.
Bist du wirklich 80 Jahr?
Ach, das ist doch garnicht wahr!
40 aussen und 40 im Herz,
zusammen 80 am dritten März!

Are you really eighty?
Surely that cannot be true!
Forty for the record, forty in your heart,
Together eighty on the third of March.

Sitting on his imposing chair, surrounded by his descendants, Louis peered at me and listened with a benign smile, while I looked up at his nose. There would be no escape from the dewdrop that day!

I saw him frequently on visits to the home of my cousins, children of his younger son Georg, with whom he lived. Louis sat at the head of the dining-table in his dark, over-large suit. The furniture was dark too and very grand, with the Danzig coat of arms crowning each chair. To the question 'how are you, great-grandfather?', he would invariably reply: '*Der Alter ist ja auch 'ne Krankheit.*' (Old age is an illness too.) He said little else and conversation only livened up once he left, immediately after the meal. His habit then was to walk to his favourite coffee house, followed by an evening visit with a carton of cakes to his mistress. One day the routine stopped.

He went out no longer, continued to sit brooding at the dining-table, depressing everyone, or went to sulk in his room. It took weeks before Georg's wife discovered the cause. On the usual visit to his mistress, with the cakes, there above her couch hung a large portrait of Adolf Hitler. It was a message so clear and awful that it put my great-grandfather off his stroke and ended his sex life forever.

Louis died in 1940. The war had broken out and everyone had either emigrated or been deported. He remained behind, left in a Jewish old people's home, and died just before the Germans shipped the old people to the extermination camps. He was reluctantly abandoned by his family but at least remained where he was born, among the memories of a long life – if that is any comfort.

'Ratz-Batz Arthur'

ARTHUR LEVANDOVSKY was my great-grandfather's nephew. He was a short, wiry man with sharp, intense eyes and the heavy eyebrows common to our family. A large nose sat between sunken cheeks and appeared to advance while the rest of his face retreated. The impression was of a bird-of-prey, best left alone. Quick with his temper and fists, he was also very strong. In later years he bore a striking resemblance to my great-grandfather.

Arthur was one of a large tribe of Levandovskys whom I barely recall, and who had intermarried with the Bosses on various occasions. There was a Jewish as well as a Catholic branch to the family. All were Kashubian horse-traders and land-owners who kept riding stables and frequently sailed to Scandinavia to sell and purchase horses.

During the First World War, Arthur, who had bandy legs and walked like a tin soldier who's horse has been removed from under him, became a Black Hussar, with a large, silver skull on his black busby and silver braid all over his uniform. The Hussars, garrisoned near Danzig, were Germany's élite cavalry regiment, sported sinister moustaches and had a fearsome reputation. In photographs of that time, Arthur looked like an extra from a Viennese operetta. But the effect is also sinister as the SS later modelled themselves on these Hussars and also dressed in black with a skull on their caps.

23

At the outbreak of the First World War, sabre in hand, Arthur rode into action with the Hussars and fought on the Western Front. Home on leave, he would recount his adventures, usually ending with 'so I slashed with my sabre and Ratz-Batz another Frenchy bit the dust!' From this time he was known in the family as 'Ratz-Batz Arthur'.

My earliest memories of Arthur in Danzig were seeing him climb trees or lampposts for a wager. If bad debts had to be collected or an insult avenged, he would settle it for a consideration. He lived in Schidlitz, a western suburb, and was the owner and *Stallmeister* of a stable in the 'Rear alley of the White Monks', a seedy street of workshops and warehouses. Twenty to thirty horses were usually in their stalls. Apart from Max who was pensioned for life, Arthur rode the horses in and out, returning from Kashubia or East Prussia with new ones and money from his sales. After a lifetime on horseback, he rode as though the animal and he were one. Many years later, when I saw Centaurs on the friezes of Greek temples, I recognised him. Some of the horses were traded to the German Army across the border, some were for the Danzig Police, others became sausage meat in Denmark. They had no names, only categories.

Max was a *Schimmel*, a white horse speckled grey. Black ones were 'ravens', a castrated horse was a *wallach*, doubtful ones were 'scarecrows'. One horse stayed for a long time, oblivious of the fact that he was known as *Miesmazel*, German-Jewish slang for bad luck of the most ominous kind.

Arthur's 'office' was a junk-room at the entrance to the stables. Furnished with unwanted carriage seats and a horsehair couch, he entertained his cronies there, as well as the local whores, who sometimes dropped by in the middle of the day for a quick break and a glass of *schnapps*. A stuffed, black eagle, bored with staring into the distance, had half-detached itself from the wall. Its gaze was now directed to the couch, were there were more interesting things to see. With its outstretched wings it was perhaps meant to represent the black eagle of the German Reich, but its beak and eyes bore a definite resemblance to Arthur.

Josef and Mango were the stable-hands who kept the horses in shape. The latter was a multiple rapist, huge, blond, with many tattoos and a broken nose. Castrated by order of the Danzig Criminal Court, he spent the week-ends in prison and his weekdays working among the horses. My cousin Peter and I would visit the stables to stock up on 'horse apples', which we valued in street-fights, as they had a great deterrent effect and could be thrown without sticking to our hands. It was also our favourite clubhouse, the place where exciting things happened. We fed the horses and the rabbits and played with Mango's goat despite her bad stench and vicious butts. When it was time to exercise the horses, we joined the stable-hands in trotting them around the yard. We also rode bareback, except when Arthur was near. 'You ride like sailor's tarts,' was his verdict, and Arthur knew a lot about sailor's tarts.

Mango was easily enraged and we took care not to get in his way, though it was always tempting to try and catch a glimpse of whatever the Criminal Court had left him to urinate with. In the afternoons he rested and at night slept in an old carriage in the corner of the yard. During his years in prison, Mango had learned to sleep with one eye open and Arthur had made him the watchman, so that at night he snored and kept an eye on the horses at the same time.

Though dilapidated, the carriage was still beautiful, made of black leather and fine wood. A built-in chest of drawers on the roof was open and chickens roosted there. On the carriage doors were the remains of the aristocratic coat of arms of Herr von Zitzewitz. I heard that it was a family trophy acquired by Arthur's father Franz-Josef, in a bet with the nobleman over which one could carry a heavier bucket of water on his rampant penis. It must have been the Levandovskys' finest hour because Arthur told the story often. Herr von Zitzewitz, convinced that the secret lay in Franz-Josef's circumcision, had rushed off to a *mohel* (Rabbinical circumcisor) to be similarly treated. One hopes that he never lost a bet again.

There was an evil-smelling pit at the side of the stables called the *Jauchgrube*, filled with accumulated horse manure and topped up with urine. It was partly covered with loose planks, on which we were careful not to tread. As small children, my cousins and I were sure that it was an entrance to hell. One afternoon, enraged shouting came from the 'office'; Mango was there quarrelling with a man who had arrived with a large dog. Suddenly both emerged. Mango was dragging the man towards the pit and after a short struggle, threw him in. My cousin Peter and I watched in panic, assuming that he had gone straight to hell or drowned on the way. The dog barked hysterically, and as we stared, two hands emerged to grab a plank, followed by the man's head, with an open knife clasped in his mouth. The dog howled as the man slowly rose up, soaked in urine, manure falling off his clothes and boots. He lunged at Mango with his knife. Mango, some distance away, had produced a butcher's knife from his riding breeches and, bending forward, made movements like a man about to scythe a field. His style looked greatly superior and we prepared ourselves to witness our first murder. The man must have thought so too, because he rushed through the yard and out, stumbling over the

26

cobblestones of the 'Rear alley of the White Monks', his dog bolting after him. Mango, knife in hand, the victor on his field of glory, spent the next few minutes howling *Fotzablecker* (cunt-sucker), a word of such complexity that I had to ask Peter for a detailed explanation. He then ambled towards the steps of the carriage to drink a bottle from his store of *schnapps*, as a thirsty man drinks water. We had learned that the *Jauchgrube* was not, after all, the entrance to hell.

Just before I left Danzig, I caught a last glimpse of Mango marching down the street in a brown uniform with a detachment of singing Nazis. He towered above the others and his voice, too, was louder than the rest. No doubt the Party would find use for a man of his talents.

Arthur and his group of cronies spent their nights in the bars and brothels of the port where sailors congregated. Some of those, the pimps among them, became Nazi stalwarts and kept a friendly and protective eye on Arthur. With their help he was later able to rescue his friends from the nearby concentration camp of Stutthof.

Once I saw him limp into the stable on a stick, with one eye bandaged. On another occasion Arthur, my father, grandfather and various cousins were arrested during a fracas in a brothel, and remained in the local lockup for a day, while a heavy and ominous silence hung over the female side of the family. By general agreement, Arthur was blamed for starting the row that brought in the police. It was convenient to blame him for most things, though no one would hold a grudge against him for long. 'Arthur, please come sober,' was the way in which invitations were usually extended to him for family meetings. Arthur would do his best, but as I frequently saw him collide against furniture on his way to the bottles, his best was not always good enough.

Among our family legends was the story of Arthur boarding streetcar No. 1, bound for Langfuhr. The passengers included a drunk, who made insulting remarks about Jews. Arthur asked the driver to evict him. 'I can't do that,' said the driver. 'If you can't, I certainly can!' said Arthur, and threw the drunk off the moving tram. The driver protested strongly, so Arthur lost his patience, threw him off as well and took the steering-stick to drive the remaining passengers down the Hindenburg Boulevard to their destination. The tram-driver picked himself up and ran off to alert the police. They collected him on their way and drove at great speed towards Langfuhr to look for Arthur and the tram. When they found him, he related his story and as the police were his drinking companions, they arrested the driver for endangering the safety of his passengers by allowing a drunk on the tram. Arthur was asked to drive the streetcar back to Danzig and did so, to the triumphant ringing of the tram bell.

The police force, most of whom were dedicated Nazis, was infinitely indulgent towards Arthur. His arrests for disorderly behaviour lasted no longer than was needed to sleep off a hangover. One night he urinated into the Neptune Fountain, a monument as dear to Danzig as Eros is to London, and indignant citizens followed a drunken Arthur and his police guard to the station. 'We pissed in the same trench on the battlefield,' said the inspector, 'and that's good enough for me.' The police report stated that Arthur had climbed up the fountain to rescue a cat, and was caught short in the process.

On the night of 12 November 1938, when Nazi stormtroopers burned down the synagogues of Langfuhr and Zoppot, Arthur guarded the Danzig Central Synagogue, club in hand, with other First World War veterans. But the police intervened and the synagogue remained intact until its 'official demolition' some six months later. Violence and arson would not have looked too well in a place located next door to Police Headquarters and the Fire Brigade.

Arthur disappeared out of my life the day before I left for England. He climbed a tree as a bet with someone, and I did not see him come down.

On my first visit to Israel, twenty years later, I was told that he was alive and in Naharia, a northern town in which the majority of the inhabitants came from Germany. When I saw him, he was still wiry and strong, asking me to punch him in the stomach with all my strength and to drop a butcher's knife onto his muscled forearm, to see it bounce off his biceps.

When the Nazis swept through Danzig into Poland, a motorcycle unit of the SS caught up with him and his horses on a country road in Kashubia. They shot the Jews among the traders on the spot, but because of the photo of Arthur as a black-uniformed Hussar and the Iron Cross he wore, they let him go. Arthur boarded an illegal immigrant ship which reached Palestine after a long and hazardous journey. With him were some of the friends he had rescued from Stutthof. Intercepted by the British, they were shipped off to Mauritius for the duration of the war. Arthur told me that he broke the nose of the British soldier who led him off the gangplank and threw another into the sea and I believe him.

During his time in Mauritius, Arthur worked as a forester. It seems that climbing trees in Danzig had been good practice for the job. He married a Polish lady there who had lost her entire family in the Holocaust. Released after five years, Arthur settled in Naharia and became the town's butcher. His hospitality to me included a large steak at a time when meat in the country was hard to find, and a generous supply of sausages when we parted.

They had a son, and it was both amazing and beautiful to see that this elderly lady and the gnarled old rowdy had produced such a handsome boy; a green branch growing from an old trunk.

Arthur was a little confused about who I was, and reminiscing about the family, said of one, 'what a beautiful girl, pity she married that Pole.' Although he didn't know it, he was referring to my parents.

Erich

As my mother was one of three sisters, Erich and Kurt Ruschkewitz, her cousins, were the only male members of her generation in our family. I have a photograph of Kurt carrying me on his back, with the Baltic sea behind us, but none of Erich to remember him by. Kurt was strong, blond and Danzig's middle-weight boxing champion. Erich, equally tall, was bespectacled and slim. A journalist, poet and later the editor of the Social Democratic newspaper *Danziger Volksstimme*, with his black hair combed back and his high forehead, he had the appearance of an intellectual at a time when every status and profession was styled for its part.

If a photograph of him did exist, it would no doubt show him with his thumb under his chin and his temple resting against his index finger. In Central Europe, it was the favourite pose of a Thinker.

Their father died young. Gassed as a soldier in the trenches, he never regained his health. My mother told me that when they were children, Erich and Kurt would appear in her home, put crystal fruit bowls on their heads and play firemen by pissing on her. As students they would cajole my grandfather for the key of his *pied-à-terre*, which he handed out if in the right mood.

It was a family secret, into which I was eventually initiated, that Erich had intimate relations with his mother, my

31

grandmother's sister. In retrospect I can understand how this might happen to a young widow with two precocious sons, competing for her love in a postwar world without men. I recall her as a coquettish lady with auburn hair, whom I could not warm to.

Kurt adored his brother, but they were also fierce rivals, possibly for their mother's affection. I remember a titanic row which I did not understand but I watched in safety between the legs of the dining-table. That table was my reading alcove when I visited the Ruschkewitz home. A large window illuminated the carpet beneath, like a stage light. Erich's library of books stretched from floor to ceiling on most walls of the house. 'Read this,' he would say, giving me Tuchholski's *Hey Ho, We Live!* or Remarque's *All Quiet on the Western Front*. I crawled under the table and absorbed them and much else, with an intensity I seldom achieved in later life.

As Nazi gangs began appearing on the streets, Kurt, the boxer, got into frequent brawls. One day, sitting at a café table, he was recognised by a group of uniformed Nazis who accosted him. 'I've never seen a "yid" fight,' said one, 'show me how!' So Kurt showed him. The man was taken to hospital. Kurt was arrested and released on bail. It was a punch to which he probably owed his life. On hearing that the Nazis planned an elaborate revenge, the family decided to ship him out to the Canary Islands, where my grandfather had business interests. Thus Kurt was saved from the fate of many others in the family. He soon became homesick, and sent for the last of his mistresses, Hildegard, a long-legged blonde who was a policeman's daughter. They were married in Santa Cruz.

I recall Kurt on a visit to Danzig, trying to persuade the family to leave before the Nazis did their worst. It was an animated debate that took place one night on the terrace of a café. In my memory, that terrace floats in no particular location, as does so much else when an adult tries to reconstruct the images of childhood. 'When you are old enough you'll visit us,' he said, when I requested details about his new home. He and Hildegard were elegantly dressed in white clothes, which hinted of the tropics, palm trees and exotic islands. It was an invitation I cherished. But the family regarded Kurt as a lightweight in all but boxing and his warnings were not heeded. He never returned.

I saw much more of Erich. For one holiday my parents rented a house in the forest, where he joined us. It rained incessantly. Surrounded by a pungent smell of damp trees and ferns, we played endless games of rummy at which I became expert in those rainy days. As the only child among grown-ups, I enjoyed the adult conversation and the scurrilous verses with which Erich improved popular hits and military marches: 'Two lads were sitting arse to arse, and farting the Radetzky March' was the relatively tame start to one, which later became more graphic.

My closeness to him was born in that time. Later, at high school, when it emerged that I was poor at Latin, Erich came to my rescue with additional lessons, until I became the Latin star of the class.

I often saw Erich sitting at the round table of his favourite café, busy with editorials, surrounded by half-smoked cigarettes and coffee cups. When the Nazis won the elections of 1935, life became dangerous for him as a socialist and a Jew. He was in hiding some of the time, at other times under arrest, and then released. One arrest followed a series of poems he wrote during the summer vacation we spent together. Published in the *Volksstimme*, they were biting in their anti-Nazi satire. He was taken to jail and beaten. His spectacles were broken on his face and his eyes were injured by glass splinters. On his release, he crossed the border to Poland and lived in my father's office in Gdynia to receive medical treatment. The newspaper Erich edited was banned, but continued to appear under different names and licenses, always a step ahead of the censors. I believe he was the first editor to apply that tactic, since then widely employed by opposition papers in authoritarian countries where a façade of legality exists.

Towards the end, the only café left to him, as Jews were excluded from all public places, was the buffet in the entrance hall of Danzig's railway station. The railways of the 'Free City' were under Polish jurisdiction, thus Nazi laws did not apply. The waiting-room buffet, with its soot-coated walls, became the last place in which Jews could sit over a cup of coffee and briefly pretend to a degree of normalcy. It was a pathetic sight and by then I was old enough to understand that.

From documents I have seen since, it emerges that towards the end, Erich represented the shrinking Jewish community in its dealings with the Gestapo. In this way an 'illegal' transport of Jews was organised with Nazi connivance, bound for Palestine. The gauleiter of Danzig wanted to demonstrate to his superiors in Berlin that by the time the city was incorporated into Germany it would *Judenfrei.*

I suspect that Erich did not join the transport out of fear that his mother could not survive the hazards of such a journey. 'Erich Ruschkewitz trusts in his star to keep him alive,' it said in the cryptic document sent by the Red Cross to Palestine at the outbreak of the war. But the 'star' failed him. While there seems to have been a grudging admiration for his courage and biting wit among the Nazis in Danzig, once the German killing machine went into action, he was swept away.

Among the few objects that remain with me from those

times is a book of poems by Erich, published in Danzig in 1929. The pages have now turned yellow. Erich was in his early twenties at the time. The book is called *Adlers Brauhaus bis Leichenschauhaus* (From the Brewery to the Morgue). Erich's last poem in this book is dedicated to his mother and called 'Final Note'. Its last lines are prophetic:

> . . . *Die Stadt mit ihren schmalen Gassen, dunklen*
> *Wegen,*
> *der alte Rathausturm mit seinen Glockenschlägen,*
> *und die See und das Haus, in dem du geboren:*
> *Alles versunken? Alles verloren? . . .*
>
> *Steh' auf! Geh' ins Café! Lass alles dir egal sein!*
> *Du wirst doch, zum Teufel! nicht etwa sentimental*
> *sein?*

The town's dark alleyways and narrow streets,
The town hall tower from which the hour beats,
The lanes you walked in, the house of your birth,
All gone forever, swallowed up by the earth.

Go out, have a coffee, don't let it matter,
To the devil with sentiment, that way it's better.

On the sunny August afternoon in 1939 when the *Kindertransport* left Danzig, it was my mother and Erich who took me to the rented bus on which I left with fifteen others. We were bound for a nearby town in Germany and would then board a train for Berlin, Holland and the Channel ferry. Two adults from the Jewish community accompanied us. At the last moment we were also joined by a member of the Gestapo, who arrived with rucksack and knickerbockers, very much out of breath and proceeded to shake hands with us as though he was somewhat late for a school outing. Erich carried the two blue suitcases which my father had bought in Warsaw a week before when I had gone to say goodbye to him. He and my mother were the last members of my family that I saw in Danzig.

As the bus drove away, they waved at me through the wire fence, becoming ever smaller until they totally disappeared from view. That is how I still remember them.

If this were a film in which such things are possible, the fence would turn to barbed wire and those who remained would disintegrate together with the entire city, until nothing remained but dust. That is indeed what happened, only it took more time and was much more terrible.

While our first daughter is named Michal after my father, the second child, had it been a boy, would have been named Arik, the Hebrew version of Erich. When we had another girl we chose Marit, in whose name there echoes a hint of him, mixed in with my mother-in-law, Miriam. I hope that Erich would approve. It was the best I could do and my daughter likes her name.

Kurt

AFTER THE WAR, Kurt, now in Spain, contacted my aunts in England to establish who had survived. I had just entered university when a letter came inviting me to visit him in Barcelona. I prepared for the journey. The British Home Office sent me a document in place of the Danzig Passport with which I had arrived. It stated that I had no nationality. I had liked the Danzig Passport, with its rampant lions and the motto that seemed a suitable admonishment for a city of merchants: *Nec Timide, Nec Temere* (Don't be slow, don't stick your neck out). With difficulty, and upon solemn assurance that I was neither a communist nor an ex-member of the International Brigade, I obtained a visa from the Spanish Consulate. Two pages of my passport were duly stamped with the slogan 'España-Great, United and Free!', which seemed somewhat at odds with the interviews I had been subjected to.

The following summer vacation, I took a train through France, bound for the Spanish border. It was to be my first journey out of England. I passed through a country recently liberated, with signs of war everywhere. The people looked drab and pale. It took a long time to pass over the temporary bridges erected next to those blown up by the retreating Germans. The journey lasted three days, with many interruptions. As postwar France had no diplomatic relations with Spain, the train stopped at the border town of Cerbère and went no further. It had been reduced by stages to one carriage, and an Italian traveller and I were now the only passengers. We descended with our luggage. It was a hot, dusty afternoon. Apart from the guard, who pointed towards a stony no-man's land, up the Pyrenees in the direction of Spain, the station was deserted. We dragged our suitcases over steep, parched terrain and, on reaching a mountain-top, saw the other side – a small white town below with the Mediterranean beyond.

As the guard had instructed we waved our handkerchiefs and sat down to wait. The Italian, who had worked as a prisoner of war in a British military canteen in Libya, spoke a little English, while I remembered my school Latin. We shook hands and introduced ourselves with the same name 'Frank', 'Franco'. Overturning a rusty steel helmet by the roadside, he sat on it and explained that he was going to Spain to find work, as there was none to be found in the postwar chaos of Italy. In the distance below, a taxi appeared and disappeared between the curves of the mountain, until it suddenly stood before us. We got in and it drove down at great speed to a Spanish border-post carved into the mountains. Half a dozen Civil Guards awaited us in olive uniforms and glossy Napoleonic hats. We must have been their first customers of the day, if not the week.

I knew them already from the poems of Lorca: 'Black patent leather hats – black patent leather souls.' Four years previously, the German-Jewish philosopher Walter Benjamin had escaped over the Pyrenees from the Germans in occupied France, and fallen into the hands of the Civil Guards at this frontier post. When told that they would hand him back to the Germans, he committed suicide.

The Civil Guards examined our papers with great attention, hoping to find a flaw, and went through every item of luggage with white-gloved hands. This finesse did not prevent the Italian from forfeiting the packets of coffee and cartons of cigarettes which he carried in lieu of money. Both of us were asked for a 'fee', which disappeared without receipt into deep military pockets. *Todo por la Patria* said a sign above their heads, 'All for the Fatherland'; but apparently not everything, after all. Content with the day's takings, the Civil Guards waved us on.

We drove down and reached the town of Port Bou. It was late afternoon, and the one train of the day had long departed. I booked a room in a small hotel. As the sun set I walked to the beach, waded through coarse, grey sand and entered the Mediterranean. It felt like returning to a home I never knew I had.

That night the little town held a fiesta. Rockets exploded over the rooftops, fireworks wheeled in the night sky and a brass band, poignantly out of tune, played the melodies to which matadors strut into the arena. The air was warm and smelt of the jasmine that gypsy women sold on the Rambla. I was celebrating my own private fiesta that night – my discovery of the Mediterranean and, as I write these lines now, I watch its waves hit the beach beneath the windows of my home.

I ran into my Italian travelling companion late in the night and tried to match him glass for glass in a bar, its floor covered with mussel shells and sawdust.

The following morning I sat on my suitcase on the train to Barcelona. The train, built in England over a century ago, rocked from side to side. It was overcrowded and the air was heavy with heat and garlic. None of this helped my hangover.

In Barcelona, Kurt's premises occupied two floors of an imposing office building previously occupied by the large

German Consulate. With the collapse of Nazi Germany
they had left in a hurry. Above its entrance, a tall metal
eagle clutched a swastika. I had no trouble guessing what
banners had hung until recently on the bare flagpoles that
flanked it. In the washroom towel-hooks bearing labels like
'Herr Schmidt' and 'Herr Kraus' had not yet been
removed and in Kurt's private office, which the Consul
General had occupied, a large rectangle of unfaded wallpaper showed where Hitler's portrait used to hang. Kurt
specialised in an impressive imitation of a raving Hitler
and whenever a Nazi on the run crossed the Pyrenees and
rushed to the nearest phone to dial the German
Consulate, the secretaries would transfer the call to Kurt.
The horrified Nazi could then hear his Führer screaming
down the phone about his 'Final Territorial Demands'.

Kurt had gained weight since I last saw him. He raised
me off the floor in a bear hug. Towering over the
Spaniards around him he was now called Don Conrado
and had prospered.

In Kurt's large enterprise, as in many other businesses
in Spain, I discovered that it was customary for one room
to be set aside for a retired officer of the Franco army, who
did nothing but sit on his laurels and draw his salary. The
regime looked kindly on this custom and remembered it
when permits and licenses had to be obtained. I had an
example of this when Kurt took me to lunch with the
Prefect of Police of Barcelona. We were received in his
spacious and elegant office furnished in beautiful
Baroque. The Prefect was a tall, grave gentleman, in a fine
uniform. A good lunch was served to us in his suite. This
was a courtesy visit, underlining the fact that a large ship-
ment which Kurt was importing would be unloaded onto
police trucks, without the inconvenience of customs and
duties. The Prefect's share in the enterprise was not

discussed. Such matters were left to underlings. Oil paintings of the Prefect's predecessors looked down from the
walls with grave understanding. Ever since, whenever I
see Tosca enter Scarpia's reception room, I know that I
have been there.

Kurt was in partnership with two brothers of impeccable
Franco connections. Their father had made uniforms for
the General in the old days when he was just a provincial
officer. The sons, reaping the benefit of the connection,
were to become synonymous with Spain's industrialisation.
Kurt's association with them gave me a curious problem
when I applied for British citizenship the following year.
The Scotland Yard inspector dealing with my file turned
the pages and casually inquired into my 'Fascist connections in Spain' in general, and Don Conrado in particular.
But as this was already the time of the Cold War and a
Fascist connection seemed preferable to a Communist one,
I was excused, though without quite convincing the
inspector of the irony of the situation.

There is a strange postscript to this, which I discovered
years later and might explain the inspector's file. My
cousin, Lottchen Kirsch, married a 'Danziger' in the
United States after the war. During the war, he had served
in US Naval Intelligence. Among his agents in Spain was a
Kurt Ruschkewitz, who transmitted information on
German and Italian shipping movements around the
Canary Islands. The name seemed familiar to him at the
time, but it was only after his marriage that he realised
who the agent had been.

The Spain I encountered was an exotic country, part
opera buffa, part tragedy. Magnificent military uniforms
abounded on the boulevards. A dozen police forces were
in evidence, plain-clothed, with hidden badges that pulled
down the lapels of their civilian jackets, or in uniforms of

varying colours and for a variety of oppressive functions. People were afraid to speak to strangers; glancing from side to side, they made a gesture with their fingers that mimed a lock on their mouths. Nazis and their collaborators who had found refuge in Spain or were on their way to disappear into Latin America, could be seen on the streets of Barcelona in brown uniforms, the stitches that so recently held their swastika armbands, still visible.

A military government propped up by the Church and the Fascist Party, dominated the land. Those who had backed the wrong side in the Civil War and still lived, did so in labour camps or begged on the streets. In matters of morality, church censorship forbade the merest hint of a kiss in films and also between married couples in public. At the same time, brothels were the accepted clubs in which gentlemen could dine, confer and amuse themselves. In the early hours of the morning they would return to their wives, mothers and unmarried sisters, all sitting together, clad in funereal black, to await the return of their *macho*. There was no divorce.

I discovered that girls of 'respectable' families, those of Don Conrado's friends, could only be invited out if accompanied by a *dueña*, a female cousin, who made certain that proprieties were observed. 'Why?' I asked Henriqueta, the beautiful daughter of Kurt's neighbour as I escorted her and a relative to a much expurgated Hollywood movie. 'Frank,' she whispered and brought her face close, 'Spanish girls are so hot, that if they are left alone with a man . . .' She lifted her hands into the air and brought her fingernails down on invisible flesh. The *dueña* nodded assent. I understood from this that she was there for my protection. (Many years later I saw that this custom was also observed in Brazil and a *dueña* invariably accompanied the girl whom one had invited. There, however,

42

the propriety had obviously been reinterpreted, since the nights were usually spent in bed with the girl and the *dueña*.)

One evening I was invited for an aperitif in a Barcelona café by a doctor who had treated me for a minor ailment. He came, accompanied by a blond man in his mid-thirties, with a cane and a limp. 'You come from the same part of the world,' said the doctor, 'and will have much in common.' I discovered that his companion came from Königsberg, a German town near Danzig, and had been a doctor in the SS. He was probably an escaped war-criminal. While our host chatted in broken German, we sipped our drinks and eyed each other, as large snakes look at small rabbits at a vegetarian lunch. When it was suggested that we drink up and proceed to a meal with ladies who were waiting elsewhere, I pleaded a prior engagement. As I left, the SS man rose and with a face that was stiff and flushed said, 'I am a soldier who came honestly by these wounds. I have nothing in common with those pigs who ran the camps.' 'You fought for the pigs who ran those camps,' I said. 'You are incapable of grasping our ideology and our integrity,' was his reply. I noticed that his emphasis was on the word 'you'. By now, our host too had realised that we had rather less in common than he thought. I walked away, turned the corner and headed for the next bar. I ordered a drink. The glass shook in my hand.

On another occasion, Don Conrado took me to lunch with the Tsarist Consul of the Russian Empire with whom Franco's Spain had the most cordial relations, thirty years after it had ceased to exist. Surrealism was an everyday event in Spain.

During the war, Franco had supported Germany and Spanish Fascist volunteers, the 'Blue Brigade', and fought with the Nazis against the Soviet Army. Franco, who had won the Civil War with the help of German and Italian troops, was repaying a debt. But when Hitler called on him to enter the war officially, he refused. Hitler henceforth referred to Franco as 'that ungrateful dwarf'. Now in the postwar era, Spain had to find its way in a world where Fascism was out of vogue.

On that first evening of my arrival we drove to the coast where Kurt kept a summerhouse. Hildegard was there to greet us. Still with wonderful, long legs and a fine figure, she enjoyed the admiration due to a tall Nordic blonde among short, dark men. The household included little white dogs, maids, and a parrot which imitated Don Conrado's German accent so well that when it called the dogs, they barked hysterically, racing around the house in search of their master, while the parrot jumped from leg to leg with glee.

Hildegard, Kurt and I got very drunk that night. It was a wake and a booze-up, in memory of those who we would have wanted with us. We toasted them one by one and, unable to move, slept it off together in one large bed.

The following afternoon, with my head still throbbing, Kurt looked me up and down and said, '*Jungchen*, your clothes are atrocious and will never do for Spain.' He was right. I wore a thick, checked shirt, corduroy trousers and heavy shoes to keep out the Manchester rain. The previous day, he had shown me his dressing-room. Standing before a large storage wall he pressed a button and the doors opened revealing long rows of suits, shirts and shoes. 'The secret of maintaining one's clothes,' said Kurt looking at mine, 'is to have so many that one never wears any too often.' It did not seem sensible advice for someone living on a modest student's grant. I began to suspect that my family's opinion that Erich had the brains while Kurt

44

had the muscle, might have been fair.

We now drove to a tailor in the nearby seaside town, Masnou. Kurt decided that I should have two white suits, two-toned shoes and white shirts. A few days later, I went for my final fitting. In the mirror, I saw a Mediterranean pimp. But this is not what worried the tailor. Something was not well with the fall of my trousers, where an awkward fold had formed from the crutch down. The tailor examined the measurements and called his colleagues. They stood around me, their chins cupped in their hands, in silent conference. Suddenly, enlightenment dawned on the face of one and with a deft stroke he flipped my testicles from right to left. The fold had disappeared. 'But this is wrong and uncomfortable,' I protested. 'That's the way it is in Spain,' came the reply, and to that I had no answer.

My white clothes were kept spotless and starched by Kurt's maid, Josefina, who addressed me as 'Señorito Frank' while I strutted about like a pimp with sore testicles. I wonder whether this difference has ever been noted in social histories and whether, silently, it plays a part in the great North-South divide. Back in Manchester, the suits were in great demand by my friends when they went to fancy-dress parties – sure enough, as pimps.

Now that I was properly dressed, Hildegard and Josefina decided that dancing lessons were next on the list for me. As Josefina came from Aragon, it had to be the *Jota*. With my arms bent over my head and the padded jacket up to my ears, I learnt to jump the intricate steps. My teachers clapped in rhythm and in a hoarse voice Josefina sang a refrain in which women were *angelitos* and men were *muy malos*. When we met in the corridors of the house she would brush against me and whisper '*oye malo!*' But I never took up the challenge.

In the days that followed I had my first Mediterranean meals and fell in love with the sun, the air, and the beautiful dark girls on the beach. All these were revelations from which I have never recovered. I also developed an affection for the language, picked up my first words while flirting on the beach with Henriqueta and her friends, and have been speaking Spanish, with pleasure, ever since.

The following week, Kurt announced to Hildegard that it was time for me to see the sights of Barcelona and that we would sleep in the apartment there. As we drove away he patted me on the shoulder and said 'now I'll do for you what your grandfather did for Erich and me!' We reached Barcelona and drove to an elegant brothel, hidden by high walls on the Avenida Generalissimo Franco. Designed for discretion, we went from the car up a private lift, to an ornate suite, where the Madam greeted Don Conrado with the courtesy due to a valued patron. His nephew too was given a very warm reception on that and subsequent nights.

The things I learned there, amid the pink plush and flashing lights, were not generally taught in Manchester and I was profoundly grateful for this unexpected legacy, the only one I ever received, however indirectly, from my grandfather, and given his reputation, the most appropriate.

My first serious lessons came from Carmen, a gypsy who worked in the brothel part-time, during peak hours. We frequently met in the evenings and went out for dinner when she was not otherwise engaged, or visited her two sisters, who sang and danced flamenco in a bar in the *Bocaria* in Barcelona's Old City. They too had worked their way up from brothels and Carmen hoped to follow, waiting for what she called '*mi oportunidad*'. She regarded her present work in the nature of an apprenticeship. 'It takes a *puta* to know life and if you don't know life you can't sing

46

flamenco.' Years later, I learnt that the opportunity had come and she had made a career in Madrid's well-known *Corral de la Moreria*. An abiding love of flamenco also remained with me from those days.

In the morning that followed our first visit to the brothel, Kurt took me to his large, elegant apartment. It included a room totally devoted to Erich and seemed to contain everything he had written or that had been written about him. On the walls were photographs, drawings and paintings made over the years by artist friends. It was a mausoleum. Kurt guided me through it, weeping bitterly while his whole body shook. To spare him embarrassment I stared at the wall and at a sombre etching of Rosa Luxemburg, lying in state after her assassination. The artist had dedicated it to Erich. I wondered how Kurt had acquired that and so much else in the room.

A year later, when my aunt visited Kurt, I learned the truth. At the outbreak of the war, shortly after I left, Erich and his mother had been arrested by the Gestapo. Kurt received this information; by using his Franco connections he could have had them both released. But it was his brother alone he wanted and Erich refused to be parted from their mother. So they went to the Death Camps and perished together, as lovers do. I could not bring myself to write to Kurt after my aunt's revelation, nor did I see him again, though I revisited Spain.

Looking back, I now understand that he could never forgive himself for his vindictiveness towards his mother and its consequences. Nor perhaps, in further mitigation, could he have foreseen the horrors of the Holocaust. It did not need my display of self-righteous indignation to punish him, nor should I have added to his agony. I only know that he died and that Hildegard returned to Germany. A sad chapter had closed for me.

A Prussian Education

A T THE AGE of six I was enrolled in a *Volksschule*, an elementary school for boys, in the Baumgartsche Gasse. It was a heavy, brick building in the Old City. Further down, where the river Mottlau flowed toward the Vistula, a tall, medieval crane, worked for centuries by prisoners, unloaded barges. In concept, the school and that treadmill had much in common. On the first day my mother waited at the school gate, holding a tall cardboard tube filled with sweets. It was the *Schultüte* given to every child on his first day. It seemed also the best day in the four years I spent there.

The *Volksschule* was a teaching factory based on fear. The cane was frequently wielded in class as well as with ceremony in the assembly hall, before the entire school, by the headmaster Herr Wentzel. For 'minor' offences, we were caned on the hands, for 'major' ones, on the rear-end. The traditionalists among the teachers had their victim's trousers brought down to the knees, usually revealing the lack of underpants. I seldom understood the reason for the canings I received. They seemed to fall at random like Acts of God. Perhaps their purpose was to give us early lessons in the Laws of Chance.

If the teachers inspired fear, Herr Wentzel, who inspired fear even in the teachers, was terror personified. Thick glass in his gold-rimmed pince-nez hid his eyes. He

wore a black suit with a stiff, white collar. An Iron Cross
hung from the lapel. At the top of his head a small quantity
of hair was parted in the centre, the rest was short bristle.
It was rumoured that if one could only smear onion on his
cane it would break in action, but I think that this was a
legend. The alternative, pushing a book into one's
trousers, only resulted in an additional caning. Our class-
teacher, Fräulein Wagner, was large, ruddy and awkward,
her attire as close to a man's as one could get while wearing a skirt. When punishment was required she sent us to
another class where the teacher – her lover, it was said –
did the job before his pupils with precision, without interrupting the lessons, or taking his eyes off the book.
Returning from him once, my 'uncle' Peter and I crouched
in the corridor in agony and discussed the possibility of
raping Fräulein Wagner in revenge. We were about seven
years old and not at all certain how one raped, but it kept
us going until the pain stopped.

Peter, as the youngest child of my grandfather's brother,
was technically my uncle and his insistence that I treat him
with due respect could be dismissed as a ploy to exact a
share of my pocket-money. We were often in trouble
together at school, on the streets, or during the tedious
services at High Holidays in the synagogue. Our expulsion
down the aisle of the synagogue, with the irate *Shamash*
(beadle) pointing his arm towards the portals, ran parallel
to the stained-glass window depicting the expulsion of
Adam and Eve from Paradise. Like a Morality Play, this
scene was repeated every year.

If I spend much time recalling punishment inflicted at
school, it is because little else happened there that was as
memorable. Our education was typically Prussian, based
on authority, obedience and fear. I learned to write in a
Gothic script called *Sütterlin*, useless for any other

language, and to reel off multiplications. I also learned something about the shape of Germany and the 'iniquities' of the Treaty of Versailles. Herr Wentzel taught this in the assembly hall, with maps that showed Germany in its Imperial glory and then after its betrayal by 'evil men': the German army had not been defeated at the Front! Venal politicians at home had stabbed the Fatherland in the back and made deals with Germany's enemies! Of these, the French were seeking revenge for their miserable defeat of 1870. The real blackguards (*die wirklichen Schurken*) were the English who stoked the fires, while the Germans and the French bayoneted each other. Though robbed now of industry, money and land, Germany would rise again to claim its rights. The last Treaty of Versailles had not yet been written! No iniquity was greater than the separation of Danzig from the German Fatherland and that too would end!

All this was the accepted myth of the time and few could grow up in Danzig without hearing about it. I heard it often from Uncle Sigmund, my grandmother's brother, who owned a saw-mill in Schneidemuhl. A great patriot, he had fought with distinction for 'Kaiser and Fatherland' on the Western Front. A serious wound left him with a mangled leg and had disabled his manhood, so that he was condemned to remain a bachelor. An ultra-conservative, Uncle Sigmund supported the Deutsch-National party and wore a modified version of the Kaiser's moustache. I learned about the heroism of the war from him and the injustices of the peace.

For my birthday he gave me a blue uniform with a steel helmet, decorated with an eagle and a spike. I was, alas, the only heir he would ever have to his patriotic zeal. On the evenings he came to dinner I was encouraged to goose-step around the house singing '*Ich bin ein Preusse, kennst du meine Fahne?*' (I am a Prussian, do you know my banner?).

It was a bitter disappointment to him therefore when, on one such visit, he saw me in bed clutching the washed-out teddy I slept with. 'You will become the laughing stock of the German army!' he shouted. 'Do you seriously imagine that soldiers go to bed clutching teddy-bears?' This news was such a shock, that I abandoned the teddy-bear forever. For many years it looked down at me with glass eyes from the top of the cupboard. His armpits were still blue, while the rest of his fur was a deathly grey. But I badly wanted to be a German soldier and so he stayed there until the armpits also faded. I have a small dog now who loves to sleep on my bed. By allowing her to do so, I am repaying an old debt. I was five years old and lucky not to become a bed-wetter as a result, but the German army probably knew how to deal with those!

It was also in that same bed that I experienced my closest encounter with a 'vision'. I awoke one night with the room in light and a total certainty that I would grow up to make objects that will give pleasure to others. As a child I could only visualise those objects as toys. It was a moment of sufficient intensity for me to recall it always in photographic detail. Uncle Sigmund would have regarded this as irrelevant to his own vision of my patriotic future, no doubt as a Grenadier on the Vistula, facing East. But I have often wondered whether it was that moment which determined my life or my life which determined that moment.

Like Uncle Sigmund, Herr Wentzel was a patriot. One day a huge, wooden image appeared in the assembly hall. It was painted field-grey with black boots, medals of silver and red, had a square head and porcine eyes. This was Field Marshal von Hindenburg, victor of Tannenberg. Two decades ago, at a village of that name not far from Danzig, he had routed and drowned two Russian armies. Now he was President of Germany and the main boulevard of Danzig was named in his honour. It was to be our sacred duty to the German 'Winter Relief Fund' to purchase coloured nails and hammer them into the Field Marshal till he turned into solid steel. I remember the occasion well. I was nine years old, had just fallen in love, and did so again each day on my way home. On a narrow street between school and home stood a Russian princess, about thirteen years old, selling pickles from a barrel. Was she really a princess? The people said so and pointed to the cellar where she lived with her father, the prince, who was hiding there in shame. The princess spoke no German, had steel-blue eyes, flaxen hair and looked extremely pale. She handed pickles to her customers with great disdain and I felt that I could watch her forever. I began to spend my pocket-money on her pickles and hoped that she would notice me. The Field Marshal therefore came at a bad time. Under the awe-inspiring glint of Herr Wentzel's pince-nez I had to convert my money into nails and hammer them in for weeks to come. Broke and ashamed, I would run past the princess pretending to be someone else. How first love burns! The experience left me with a lasting passion for pickles.

There were many other Russians in Danzig. Some had escaped from the purges and were passing through, others stayed and worked in Danzig's oldest profession, trade between East and West. Red sailors on shore leave would reel around the harbour at night or call from the portholes of their vessels for girls to come aboard and 'taste their borscht'. One day, a boy from my class took me home and told me to follow him up a ladder to a gabled attic. It was an old merchant's house, full of unexpected angles and niches, in one of which stood a life-size Madonna. A circular window overlooked the rooftops of the city. On a camp-bed a naked girl and a Russian naval officer lay together totally drunk. The wooden floor was strewn with empty bottles, her fur coat and his dark blue uniform. The smell of *schnapps* met us at the ladder. We tiptoed to the bed. I had never seen a naked girl apart from my cousin, Lottchen Kirsch, when, stark naked with a cushion between her legs, she had jumped about playing 'horse', but she was my age and that didn't count. The man groaned, turned from the girl and seemed about to open his eyes. We rushed back toward the ladder, bottles rolling behind us. There were many things I wanted to ask, but suddenly felt very grown up and knew that men of the world don't ask questions. One thing was certain, I learned more on the streets and in the houses of Danzig than in the *Volksschule*.

A year later the wooden as well as the real Field Marshal was replaced by Adolf Hitler, and most of my friends and teachers took to wearing Nazi uniforms. It was 1936. The Nazis had won the elections some months before and were ready now to settle accounts with those who had not joined their ranks. Both Fräulein Wagner and Herr Wentzel belonged to the Deutsch-National Party of my Uncle Sigmund. They were dismissed and one night Herr Wentzel was so badly beaten that he lost an eye. 'Pure terror' was human after all.

My mother now decided that I must learn to defend myself against beatings from the Hitler Youth, some of whom loafed around the streets looking for Jewish children. I was instructed to go to an elegant villa belonging to her friends, on the long avenue that had changed its name from 'Hindenburg Boulevard' to 'Adolf Hitler Boulevard'. (It is now named 'Victory Boulevard' in Polish

Gdansk.) The owner was a wealthy tobacco merchant who had acquired a boxing instructor for his son. I did not know the boy well, but he had once impressed me by taking a roll of peppermints and spitting them over the bushes of his garden to see how far they could fly. A boy who could do that with sweets obviously had very rich parents. It was my first glimpse of conspicuous consumption. In the graceful house, a boxing ring had been erected and I was given gloves. The boy must have had quite a few lessons already and I assume that the instructor saw me as a suitable punchbag for his pupil. It did not take long before he landed a straight blow into my face. I saw black, and my nose bled. The central cartilage was broken and I have been breathing through one and a quarter nostrils ever since. I did not wait to get a cauliflower ear as well. On the few occasions that Hitler Youth chased me, I either ran or fought dirty without the restraints of Marquis of Queensberry rules.

From this time on, I also sporadically attended a Jewish youth club, called 'JJB', situated in a run-down building, near the shipyards. Other children, regular attendants there, were rehearsing plays, hearing lectures and preparing excursions into the country. There was great excitement too over a coming trip to Finland. I drifted in and out, admired the girls who seemed so grown up, but I found no focus there. Once, on a dark winter evening, another boy and I explored the fences of the shipyards, found a hole and gorged ourselves sick on coconut shells that had spilled out of sacks on the quayside. Known later as the 'Lenin Shipyards', they were to have their place in history.

One memorable event occurred one early evening in 1937. On entering the club-house I was told to go to the cellar where our youth-leader, Fritz Gershon, and other

54

children were standing before a man squatting in the
shadows. A fugitive from Spain, he was a German member
of the International Brigade, had stowed away in a vessel,
reached Danzig, and was trying to get to the Soviet Union.
To view us better, he held the broken frame of his glasses
against his face. He looked exhausted and terrified. I
recall his domed, moist forehead, sparse hair at the sides
and a goatee beard. He looked the prototype revolution-
ary of the time, part Lenin, part Trotsky, part Jewish intellectual. It was a face more at home in a public library than
peering through a gun-sight in a Spanish trench. Perhaps
he was hiding in the club-house near the Vistula to wait for
a Russian ship. With hindsight one knows that, had he
reached his destination, he would have been killed at
Stalin's orders, or handed over by the NKVD (Soviet
Secret Police) to the Gestapo, as a gesture of fraternal
friendship. We gave our pocket-money to Fritz, so that the
man could proceed towards his likely death. Fritz
Gershon, who was the type of older boy younger boys
would like to become, had, alas, a similar fate awaiting
him. He was shot by the Germans at the outbreak of the
war.

In my last school year, the entire class was marched off
to the cinema. The Nazis were inventing screen heroes
and all the children of Danzig were sent to admire them.
A street rowdy called Horst Wessel, was one. Later, in
England, a German refugee who knew him from home
told me that Horst had been a pimp and that his death was
related to his career rather than his politics. With such
qualifications, he plainly embodied all the Nazi virtues and
their battle-hymn was named in his honour. The film dealt
with street fights and intrigues between heroic Nazis and
vicious Bolsheviks, ending with the death of Horst. There
was a similar theme to *Hitler Youth Quex* which we were also

taken to see. I only recall the grand finale with swastika banners, fanfares and drums. 'Our banners to the fore, we march towards the future man by man,' sang the uniformed masses, as they goose-stepped into the horizon. This technique became the favourite cliché of totalitarian regimes everywhere. Its prime Nazi exponent was Hitler's favourite film-maker, Leni Riefenstahl. Brilliant, corrupt and tough, she outlived her patrons, to photograph tribes in Africa whom her fellow Nazis doubtless would have exterminated.

I completed my four years at the *Volksschule* as one completes a stretch in prison, coming out with almost as little to show for it. I have read that a Prussian education was thorough and effective for all its authoritarianism. Hegel, after all, praised it highly. Perhaps this was true of the next stage at high school or *Gymnasium*, where the children of better families studied for another seven years. On photographs I have seen of them, groups of self-assured boys with smart, embroidered caps, look towards the camera, as one looks towards a certain future. In the photograph I have of our class, only Fräulein Wagner looks aggressive. The rest of us crouch there with embarrassed smirks and shifty eyes. *Esprit de corps* was not something we had heard of.

The majority of children stayed at the *Volksschule* for two more years and were then released into the streets. I was not to have the benefit of either system, as the government of the Free City of Danzig decreed that Jewish children were henceforth barred from all schools.

Uncle Fimek and Mr Gold

My FATHER CAME to Danzig with his younger brother, my uncle Fimek, who worked in the transport business my father founded. Called 'Transit Lloyd', its large trucks hauled merchandise between the port and the Polish hinterland. The offices were in the centre of the city, the staff half-German, half-Polish and there was Fimek, shouting down the phone to Warsaw, or else in Warsaw shouting back.

From conversations I overheard and the exotic samples that crowded his room, I knew that in addition to Transit Lloyd, he was busy with other deals and a whole range of 'once-in-a-lifetime' opportunities. Principal among these was 'the picture of the triple image'. This was made of folded cardboard, so that standing directly before it one could admire a landscape, while on one folded side there appeared a nude and to the other, a man playing a violin. Fimek referred to it as a 'Revolution in Art' and sold the rights to a Polish company who, disappointingly, adapted it to display the photographs of Poland's governing triumvirate. Henceforth from many Polish shop-windows the three could be seen merging imperceptibly into each other as one walked past; two bellicose generals and a sad man in a tuxedo. Fimek claimed to have been cheated in the deal, which may be the reason why no revolution in art resulted from the 'triple image'.

My family in Danzig were permanently bemused by Fimek from the time he became an 'in-law'. He was a smart dresser, with a white flower in his buttonhole, a neatly rolled umbrella *à la* Chamberlain and spats. He also had an unfocused 'lazy' right eye. Though he knew German, Polish and Russian, there was something unfocused too in his manner of speaking. To the German side of the family he was the quintessential Polish *Luftmensch* (a man of empty promises), confirming all their prejudices of the *Ostjuden* (the Jews of the East). He pinched cheeks, patted shoulders, promised something magnificent, asked for a small advance and reappeared weeks later with a new scheme, his enthusiasm as fresh as his flower.

There was the matter of the Warsaw taxi-cabs. My grandfather Franz had a Polish mistress whose husband proposed to Fimek a joint venture for the purchase of Warsaw's first taxi-cabs. Until then horse-drawn *droshkys* were the usual means of transport. The time had come to modernise. My grandfather would finance the cabs, while his mistress's husband would stay in Warsaw to manage them. It seemed an ideal arrangement for everyone. To be just, Fimek had no part in the débâcle that followed. The lady's husband ran the taxi-cabs, which progressively vanished and reappeared again under a new name, doing well. When my father was asked to travel to Warsaw and investigate the mystery, he discovered that the husband was also the owner of the new company and, in exchange for letting matters rest, promised not to drag my grandfather through a divorce scandal. It was one of the world's oldest traps in which Fimek had innocently helped to plant the cheese.

Many years later, walking with my mother's sister, Ruth, along Oxford Street in London after the war, I was suddenly dragged across the road by her. She had seen the mistress and her husband strolling arm in arm in our direction.

My mother had a cold loathing of Fimek; he was the alter ego of the sophisticated man she married, to whom he was diametrically opposed and yet resembled. Fimek had a passion for Argentinian tangos which he whistled incessantly. If ever I began to whistle, my mother would shout 'Stop sounding like your uncle!' Whenever I find myself whistling now, I think of them both and stop.

In 1935 my father and Fimek had to escape from Danzig. During a routine visit to a Nazi police official, whom my father knew, the man left his room long enough for my father to see a list, upside down, of Polish Jews about to be arrested. His name was on it. The official came back. 'We may not see each other for a while,' he said, and returned the list to its dossier.

The Nazis were about to strike a blow at Polish business interests as well as the Jewish community, with the arrest of dozens of businessmen that night. After warning friends, my father and Fimek crossed into Poland and never returned.

I saw Fimek again in Warsaw on visits to my father, wheeling and dealing as always. I noticed that his flower had changed to red. He was now busy marketing rubber shoelaces, which, because of their elasticity, saved their owners the trouble of bending down to tie them.

I went to Warsaw for the last time just before the war, to bid my father farewell before leaving for England. He took me on a round of cousins: ladies whose hands had to be kissed and men who wanted to know about Danzig and the Nazis at first-hand. Sadly, they were soon to know more than I could tell them.

I was shown the sights of the city by Fela, a very pretty relative, who had once been with us in Danzig and at the seaside in Zoppot. She was a little older than I, with green eyes and auburn hair and light years ahead in *savoir-faire*. When the war broke out, her parents left Warsaw for their hometown, Bialistok. There the Germans killed them. Hidden by farmers for three years, Fela survived. When the Red Army routed the Germans and entered Poland, Fela's uncle, her father's brother, was one of the Russian officers. An engineer in Moscow, he had been a student there during the 1917 Revolution and unable to leave, married and settled in the Soviet capital. Searching for his family in Bialistok, he discovered Fela, took her to the Soviety Political Commissar, newly appointed to the district, and asked for travel papers permitting her to join his family in Moscow. The Commissar sat behind his desk and shook his head. 'It is impossible.' Fela relates that her uncle removed his pistol from its holster, placed it on the Commissar's table and said, 'You see this? With it I'll shoot you, then the girl, then myself.' There was a long silence, broken by the Commissar who said, 'Well of course, on the other hand . . .' And so Fela went to Moscow. She lives in Copenhagen now.

Of all the relatives I met, and of those I did not meet, on that side of the family, Fela alone survived. By her count, they numbered more than one hundred. They are now a part of the facile phrase 'six million', which disguises so many faces and so many hopes. I can still see some of those faces.

My mother had sent me off to Warsaw with a list of clothes which I would need in England. My father and Fimek dutifully took me to a tailor where I soon began to look ridiculous in long flannel trousers and jackets *à l'anglaise*. Uncle Fimek even designed a blazer for me; blue with vertical yellow stripes. As a natty dresser himself he knew what was 'genuinely English'. On reaching England

I also discovered a dozen pairs of rubber shoelaces in my suitcase, which might have lasted a lifetime had I worn them.

Based on the only Englishman I had met, I had the worst suspicions of England. A sandy-haired official at the British Consulate in Danzig, he looked bleached and wore a prickly green jacket that seemed to be made of cactus skin (I later learned it was Harris Tweed). His responses to my mother's questions were so languid that the pauses between his sentences assumed more significance than anything he conveyed. I recall staring up at his gaunt figure and counting the seconds that passed in the intervals between his words.

My clothes were packed into two blue suitcases, bargained for in Nalewki Street, the main shopping area of the Jewish district. I had sulked there in a corner among the half-sewn luggage, hating the bargaining, which was not 'done' in Danzig, but which Fimek, my father and the shopkeeper so relished. (In the future I would be punished for this fastidiousness, in Istanbul, Caracas and again in postwar Warsaw, where I know that the bargaining game is expected and I silently overpay). The transaction in Nalewki Street was interrupted by air-raid sirens. It was only a test, but hundreds of people rushed into the street shouting in Yiddish *'Milchume! Milchume!'* (War!). They were a week too early.

As we walked down a main street with my suitcases, we saw a man slumped against a wall; his back was turned to us and we could see between his parted legs that he was spitting blood. My father spoke to him. The man replied in German. He had escaped from a concentration camp, hidden in a freight train, crossed the border and seemed now to be dying on his feet in Warsaw. My father gave him money and we passed on in shocked silence. Later that day

I saw a street orchestra of Jewish children, in black gabardines and side-locks, playing for coins on a crowded boulevard. One instrument was a long toothless saw which a boy twisted and turned while using his bow. It was poignant music, very sad then and sadder now. In later life, as a sculptor, I have often been tempted to depict the scene of that little orchestra but as I know that it would only result in parody not in truth, I leave it cast in my mind.

I left Warsaw by train, seen off by my father and Fimek. Before the train left, my father asked Fimek to bring me a magazine and when he had gone said: 'Whatever happens from here on, study hard, go to university and don't be like your Uncle Fimek.' Fimek returned with magazines and the train drew out. I had seen my father for the last time. In what followed I studied hard, went to university and tried not to be like my Uncle Fimek. Perhaps I even tried too hard.

With the outbreak of war I heard nothing of Fimek. In my mind he was bracketed with the fate of my parents for whom I had reason to fear the worst. But in my first year at Manchester University, shortly after the war, I received a letter that had been stamped, returned and restamped a number of times. It came from the American Occupation Zone of Germany, and its sender was a 'Mr Gold'. It took time before I realised that it was Fimek under a new name. I replied at once and contacted my aunts, his sisters, in New York, who wrote back that they were in touch with 'Mr Gold' and that he would soon reach the United States.

Over a year later, I visited the United States for the first time to spend the summer with my aunts and cousin. There I met Fimek again and heard his story. At the outbreak of war, Poland was attacked by Germany and the

Soviet Union who between them carved up the country. Fimek happened to be in the area the Russians occupied. While they were busy killing and deporting vast numbers of the Polish population to Siberia, Fimek managed to convince a Commissar that he was Russian and received permission to travel to Moscow. It seems that the Soviet Union was no match for Fimek. On his arrival in Moscow he moved in with his father's cousin, the same man who during the war was to find Fela in Bialistok.

Fimek soon found work as the production manager in an armaments factory. The management's task was to fulfil a monthly quota determined by a distant ministry. Failure resulted in dismissal and once the war broke out, in being sent to the Front. It took more than mere hard work to achieve the quota as there was a chronic shortage of all the parts needed to manufacture the product. Fimek became the salvation of the management. The required parts might be made in Tashkent which, Fimek would discover, suffered from a severe shortage of soap. Soap was churned out in another part of the Soviet Union where new underpants had not been seen in months. Those were made in the Urals which suffered from a desperate shortage of socks. Fimek rushed around the Soviet Union with two railway carriages, exchanging socks for underpants, pants for soap and soap for the vital spare parts the factory needed. The management of other factories were sent to the Front but he and his colleagues remained, achieving more than their monthly quota. His method was so effective that Stalin awarded the Order of Lenin to the factory for its outstanding example of 'Socialist Labour'. Fimek had not spent a lifetime on the rough side of capitalism in vain.

He would have risen high in the Establishment but towards the end of the war Fimek was made staff officer, with a rank of colonel, to a general participating in the final push into Germany. On his way he saw Danzig reduced to rubble by Russian bombs and shells and reached Berlin to act as the general's interpreter and *aide-de-camp*. The general had style. Fimek described their entry into Berlin in a column of glistening, open Mercedes cars, looted on the way. The general sat in the front and on reaching the centre of Berlin, graciously threw Iron Crosses, Knights Crosses, Eagles and Swastikas, which he kept in sacks at his feet, towards the inhabitants, like a Grand Signior distributing largesse. They had been stripped off German prisoners in huge quantities and the general felt that this disgraced paraphernalia and the German people deserved each other. Nobody dared to pick them up.

By the time Fimek received orders to return to Moscow he had made other plans. He changed into civilian clothes, hid the valuables he had acquired in Germany, entered the American Sector as 'Mr Gold' and identified himself as a 'displaced person'. He stayed in a transit camp and waited there until his sisters could bring him to America. Meanwhile the Russians were looking for him and had they found him he would have been shot as a deserter. As they failed in their search, the KGB in Moscow harassed and interrogated his uncle for years, in their attempt to locate Fimek.

In 1985 I visited Moscow with my daughter Michal. We first stayed in Copenhagen with my cousin, Fela, who had seen much of Fimek in Warsaw and later in Moscow. I was shaving before leaving for the airport, when she came into the bathroom and whispered urgently: 'If the KGB ask whether you know Fimek Meisler, deny everything!' I was as close as I ever got to a major shaving accident. But there was to be no high drama when we arrived at Moscow airport some hours later, and the KGB officials contented themselves with confiscating our copy of *Rolling Stone* magazine.

When I saw Fimek in New York in that summer of 1948, he had not been long in the USA, but he had not been idle. His first enterprise was smuggling second-hand cars from the USA to Brazil and he had made a good profit. Now he was purchasing Brownstone houses near Central Park and busy evicting tramps and unfashionable painters, squatting in his new properties. He barely spoke three sentences of English but then he never needed a language to get along. He converted the houses into luxury apartments with a sure instinct for the needs of postwar New York. Much of it was financed by the valuables he had acquired in Germany. 'If I had been here fifteen years ago I would own half of New York by now,' he told me. He certainly would have owned a large slice of it. All this must have been light relief compared to his activities in the USSR and Germany.

In the years that followed, in many parts of the world, I met people who had known Fimek. I always flinched then, waiting for the inevitable and it never failed to come. They had been arrested, sent to Siberia, landed themselves with a trainload of defective army caps, lost their money, were still waiting for the promised fortune or had been deported somewhere along Fimek's path. According to a half-Jewish relative who had been hidden throughout the war by the German officer who was her uncle, Fimek suddenly appeared in Passau, Bavaria, where they were living after the Nazi collapse. It was the Autumn of 1945. He was in civilian clothes and stayed for three months. 'Had he deserted?' I asked. 'No, but he was hiding and he was busy.' 'What did he do?' 'He was selling guns.' 'Rifles?' 'No, artillery and tanks.' 'But to whom?' She had been too young to know. 'Perhaps Czechoslovakia.' Looking at the map I saw that Passau was not far from the Czech border.

For such an enterprise Fimek would have needed a considerable organisation behind him. Could it have included 'the general who had style'? In retrospect could his original appointment as aid to that general have been more than a coincidence? Could his talents have been spotted in his Moscow days by others? I began to understand why my cousin in Copenhagen had been anxious about me at the Soviet border.

During my stay in New York, I once joined Fimek for dinner at the home of friends he knew from Russia. Their name was Sobel. Much of the conversation that evening was in Russian, of which I understood little.

In 1957 a photographer working in New York's Greenwich Village was arrested by the FBI and exposed as Colonel Rudolph Abel of the KGB. He was found to head a network of agents gathering information about US rocket technology. Among his agents were Fimek's friends, the Sobel brothers. While Colonel Abel was in time extradited to the Soviet Union, the Sobels were sentenced to life imprisonment. Some years before they had made a deal with Beria, head of the KGB, to spy for the Soviet Union in exchange for permitting them and their families to emigrate to America. At some point Beria had called in his debt.

During the interrogation, the FBI investigated their circle of friends and found that 'Mr Gold' was also, in fact, a Russian officer living in New York under a false name. It seemed a great coup, ripe for the headlines, in those days of Senator McCarthy. I don't know how Fimek succeeded in convincing them that he was not a Soviet spy, but the eternal survivor interested in no other cause. In the end, they believed him and he was released.

A few years later Fimek had become a solid citizen. He married a lady he knew from Russia and promoted the planting of trees in his neighbourhood. He might have run for mayor but one day his heart gave out and he died suddenly.

Sometimes I saw glimpses of my father in him and once he looked at me and said, 'You have your father's hands.' We never got on, perhaps because he also saw my mother in me, while I saw him mainly through her eyes. But of all the family, he alone was built to survive those murderous times. No killing machine had been built in Germany or in Russia fast enough to catch up with Uncle Fimek. He died in his own time, on his own property, among the saplings he raised, in the Manhattan of his dreams.

At times it seems that I hear someone whistling an Argentinian tango and were I to raise my head, I would see Fimek's spirit just above the clouds on its way to clinch a deal in China.

Ilse

M Y RECOLLECTION of my father's escape from Danzig, was a hurried leave-taking in the night. I awoke to see him dressed in a winter coat and hat, and remained in bed half-asleep, sensing tension, but unaware of the danger he faced. He crossed the border, hidden in one of his trucks which was loaded with merchandise from Danzig's harbour, bound for Poland. Hidden in another truck, Fimek crossed the border in the same manner. My mother told me that the police arrived early in the morning to arrest him, but I slept through their search.

I can only understand, in retrospect, how sad it must have been for him and how much this parting was to change our lives. My father never returned. He rebuilt his business in Poland in the few years that remained before the outbreak of the war that killed him. To visit him we travelled across the border to Gydynia or Warsaw. My mother did not want to live in Poland and from then on there was an estrangement between my parents.

Shortly after his departure, my mother and I moved. The black humour of coincidence placed us next door to one of the leading Nazi Party bosses of Danzig. He was a dark, slim man, with a short, plump wife. Their only child was Ilse, a little older than me. An impressive car would take him to Nazi headquarters in the morning and he strutted towards it in a brown uniform, flipping a horsewhip against his boots.

Ilse and I frequently played together in our flat or hers. Like her mother, she was plump and pleasant, nicer to me than I was to her. What my mother or her parents thought of this friendship I never knew. We played charades using her father's array of peaked caps, jackboots and uniforms, brown and green for hunting, and his collection of decorative daggers, which one sees nowadays in shops of Nazi memorabilia. Under Ilse's direction we rehearsed excerpts from *Der Rosenkavalier* and other operettas, in which a hero in uniform is always centre-stage. 'When you give roses in Tyrol, there's just one meaning to it all,' sang Ilse in a full voice, one hand on her heart, one knee on the floor. My contribution sounded less promising.

Once Ilse's father was made responsible for organising a political rally, in an open stadium outside town, where an important Nazi official from Berlin was to address the crowd. With little bits of paper on the carpet, Ilse and I helped him to work out the seating arrangements.

I remember her father recounting his 'heroic days', the street-brawls with Socialist and Communists during which he once harangued a crowd from a platform, blood dripping from his bandaged jaw. Those had been the hard days and now it was time for him to reap the rewards of victory.

Goebbels had come to Danzig to campaign for the Nazis at the elections, some months before. Ilse's father had been responsible for the receptions, the banners, garlands and motorcades. He and his wife were still basking in that success. By strange coincidence, my cousin, Hans Boss, learning carpentry before emigrating to Palestine, worked for a master-carpenter who constructed the obelisks, crowned with eagles, lining the Langgasse for this parade. The carpenter was a Communist and his son, who hammered away at the project, with my cousin, was later to become a Minister in the East German Government. 'How right my father was!' he wrote on a postcard, mailed from postwar Danzig to my cousin in Israel. It was a reminder of his father's predictions that in the end 'the Nazis will disappear and the Communists will take it all!'

One Sunday, Ilse asked me to join the family on an outing. We left in an open car stopping for ice cream on the way. Our destination was the country house of a Nazi colleague. In his orchard, a picnic lunch and other guests awaited us. The host was currently under a shadow in the Party for suspected corruption and had been suspended from his functions. Perhaps he had been reaping too many of the fruits of victory too soon. After the meal the adults listened sympathetically as he spoke of unrewarded loyalty. The children went off to play. There was a moment of consternation when we decided to be soldiers in the Spanish Civil War and I realised that they were on the Fascist side. I insisted on being a Republican and was loyally supported by Ilse.

While we played checkers on the carpet of their living room, Ilse's father, who felt that he had attained the eminence ripe for autobiography, but could barely spell, would call to us from his study. 'Ilse, how do you write FIST? Frank, how do you spell PLATFORM?' We would dictate to him without interrupting our game.

Ilse's father liked to entertain the family with party songs and sentimental ballads at the piano, which stood in the living room. Occasionally there were late-night beer sessions with cronies from the Party. One night their singing was so late and loud, that my mother sent me next-door to ask for quiet. Dressed in pyjamas, I rang the bell, walked up to Ilse's father at the piano and delivered the message. There was no sign of Ilse or her mother. The living room was full of men in brown breeches, vests and braces; it reeked of beer fumes and cigar smoke. I remember the song I interrupted: 'Comrades, Soldiers, Hang the Jews, Put the Bigwigs to the wall – Kill them all.' They were beating time to the music with improvised drums, using pot-lids as cymbals. Ilse's father was drunk and it took him some time to focus on me. There was silence as the piano and the singing faltered. 'Give your mother my regards,' he said after a while. 'We'll keep it low. Don't want you to be late for school.' I walked back to our flat. The music stopped. Ilse's father bore no grudge and said when next I saw him, 'Old comrades and old songs are the spice of life.' And then, as if confiding a secret to an adult, added, 'Those shitheads in black will ruin it all.'

When Fritz emigrated to the United States, we moved to his flat on the 'Lane of the Woolweavers'. It was some distance from Ilse's home and I never met her again. Once I saw her father in his uniform, coming down the stairs of the Town Hall. It must have been an official function as he looked dapper, with his hand on a decorative dagger. He winked at me in recognition. 'How is Ilse?' I asked. 'She is at summer-camp. Is your mother well? Kiss her hand for me,' and he marched on towards his car.

I wonder where Ilse is today. If I can suspend the judgement of an adult and revert to being a child, I wish her well and hope that she has had a good life. As an adult I have to add that shortly after the war I saw Ilse's father in a newspaper photograph. He had been executed in Poland for war crimes. He hung from gallows, hands tied behind his back, his feet pointing inwards, his head down, like a naughty schoolboy being scolded.

Kashubs and Kashubia

SOUTHWEST OF DANZIG, within the 'Polish Corridor', lay the Kashubian countryside, hilly farmland, lakes and forests. The Kashubians are a Slavic people with a language of their own, a remnant of the Slavic tribes who, in the distant past, inhabited much wider areas of present-day Germany. Wedged now between Germany and Poland they were the third-class citizens of whichever side held these borderlands. They had been taxed and treated with contempt by Teutonic Knights, Poles, Prussians and Germans. In my childhood they were under the Poles once again.

Their only desire was to be left in peace to farm their land and trawl for fish along the sandy, waterlogged coastline of the Baltic. Karthaus (Cartuzy) was their capital, a small, unremarkable market town, with a Carthusian Church from which it received its name. My great grandmother, Rosa, was born there.

Kashubian peasants drove to Danzig regularly to sell their produce from carts and stalls in the 'Kashubian Market', in the poorer part of the city. Some had 'bettered' themselves, settling in Danzig and in time were absorbed into the German-speaking population.

I had a friend living in the 'Hundegasse', whose parents had left Kashubia for Danzig and I spent a great deal of my time in their home. The father was a tailor. There were two children in addition to my friend Bubi (Joachim) Szerszewski and we all got along well. Bubi's sister Gisela was a little younger and we would occasionally cuddle and kiss with great innocence, when there was an opportunity. Sometimes we were spotted by the youngest, Friedel, who had a price for everything and the price of his silence was marzipan. Not just any marzipan, but white hearts with soft centres and crystallised fruit, or better still 'Ducat-shitters'. We walked in silence to the Long Market, near the Green Gate, to the shop that specialised in them. The 'Ducat-shitter' was a little man, with an intense expression, made of marzipan, straining to eject a large, gold-covered chocolate ducat from his buttocks. Friedel had the habit of biting his head off, pocketing the ducat and silently handing me the rump. We had a deal and I learned that there was a price for every pleasure. I hope that Friedel survived the war and became what he was plainly meant to be – a very smart businessman.

Bubi, with his mother's dark hair and strong nose, was bony and tall for his age. Friedel and Gisela had inherited their father's delicate build and sandy hair. When Bubi and I fought or wrestled, experimenting with Nelsons and double-Nelsons like the great wrestlers who came to Danzig and whom we stalked for autographs, he carefully removed his glasses, revealing squinting eyes and a red welt on the bridge of his nose. Fighting with other boys, when there was no time for such refinements, he invariably protected his face by a pre-emptive strike, aided by his long arms and a mounting rage. An effective technique which I soon copied from him.

Mr Szerszewski told us about the war and the time he spent in the trenches in France. We heard tales about soldiers whose hair turned white after gas attacks and about the little dark men from Fiji who slid, naked and oiled, into German lines at night, cut the soldiers' throats and were rewarded by their British officers for the ears they carried back. On the day the war ended Mr Szerszewski had fallen onto the upright bayonet of a soldier lying dead in the mud. A long scar, roughly stitched, ran diagonally across his stomach and had to be encased in elastic bandages. The wound caused him agony whenever the weather changed.

Bubi and I built railways with improvised parts and laid wooden tracks throughout the house to run them on, sometimes even out of the fourth-floor window. We also collected leeches from the muddy banks of the Radaune, a lazy river that flowed through town. The elderly pharmacist to whom we sold them, Herr Berger, had his shop in 'Paradise Lane'. He was grossly fat, and always wore the same brown suit, the tie hidden by a triple chin. The shop was saturated with the smell of his pipe tobacco and the urine he analysed in a small, side-room laboratory. 'Why read hands when one can read piss?' we heard him say to a visitor. 'I can tell you more about this town than the palmists, priests and cops combined.'

We came to him with our jar of leeches, our hands and shoes covered in mud – I don't remember a time when my bare knees did not have scars and scabs in various stages of healing. Herr Berger was pedantic about his worms and with a magnifying glass selected only the best. Once we asked him how he knew which to pick. 'If you were a couple of leeches,' he said, holding up his magnifying glass in our direction, 'I'd throw you back into the Radaune.'

This source of livelihood had often brought us into territorial conflict with other boys searching for leeches. Our defensive technique was to flail with both hands amid the mud, while protecting our jars and leech-sticks. No words were exchanged and after a while it was accepted that we were legitimate collectors.

One day in 1939 we arrived with our leech jars and found the shop boarded up. The pipe smoke and the urine lingered about the door but Mr Berger had emigrated. We returned to the Radaune and ceremoniously poured the leeches back. Our plan now was to make money from postage stamps. The government was printing colourful new ones, which displayed eminent citizens and vessels built in the Danzig shipyards. We believed that the dull stamps of old would soon have collectors' value and give us an income for which we would not have to wrestle in the mud. But the war intervened.

In the winter we ice-skated on a frozen river or sneaked into the cinema. My grandfather had owned some in his heyday and the lady in the box-office of the Schauburg Cinema who seemed to know something about me, allowed us to sit in the empty pit, where the piano still stood from the days of the silent movies. Perhaps she had been one of my grandfather's many girlfriends. We sat staring at the screen that flickered with black streaks, and quarrelled over which one of us was in love with the actresses who sipped champagne, loved, and sometimes died vertically above us. That my eyesight had been ruined by this proximity was discovered on the day I sat in the real auditorium and needed my grandmother's pince-nez to see Shirley Temple on the screen. From then on I wore glasses like Bubi.

We ice-skated on a narrow waterway, where dense reeds covered both banks. It passed along poor neighbourhoods and at dusk, when it was difficult to see the ice ahead, gangs of children lay in wait among the reeds and having strewn a barrier of dirt, waited for the skaters to fall. They rushed out from their hiding-places, and sat on the fallen skaters, while others removed the skates as well as the boots. Running through the reeds, they disappeared in the dark. It was agony to hobble home barefoot, on ice and through frozen streets. We had met boys howling in rage and pain on that route. We therefore skated with knuckle-dusters in hand, ready for the gangs and their traps. To keep up courage and appear more formidable we hollered marching songs: 'The rain sweeps through the meadows and the tents in which we lie. The Kaiser pays us money and we march off to die.' We passed barriers of dirt and often fell, but were never attacked. Half a lifetime later, in war, combing through apricot orchards for Egyptian commandos, with a gun instead of a knuckle-duster, I could think of no better way to keep up courage than by singing those songs. My fellow soldiers and perhaps the Egyptians hiding there must have thought me unhinged, but it worked yet again.

Mrs Szerszewski had a younger sister, Sosia, who worked in a sailors' bar and supplemented her living by supplying further hospitality after hours. I saw her at the house on evening visits, sometimes cheerful, with chocolates for the children, but more often she would be drunk. There were hysterical rows then between her and Mrs Szerszewski, in which no one interfered yet all listened. The sister had an attractive, round face with big dark eyes, curled hair and wore a fur coat of nondescript colour. During these rows, she was on the defensive, mascara ran down from her eyes and she swayed in grief, while Mrs Szerszewski accused and attacked. Most of it was in Kashubian and it was sad and distressing to see. One day Bubi told me that his aunt had died. I was shocked but not surprised and asked no questions. 'Come to the wake,' he said, 'tomorrow.'

The house was full of mourners, with more arriving from the countryside on horses and carts. They came with baskets of blood-sausage, smoked eels and cheeses wrapped in green leaves, which were piled onto the long tables already stacked with bottles of vodka. The farmers wore dark suits, the women their Sunday cotton dresses. Barefoot, they put on shoes only when they reached the house at the 'Hundegasse'. The guests ate in formal fashion, toasting the deceased and praising her good nature and warm heart. But the vodka soon took effect and they began to sing sad Kashubian dirges:

> 'All the little fish sleep in the sea,
>   Truala Truala La,
> Only my old woman won't let me rest,
>   Truala Truala La.'

A small, dapper German, in a light suit, who played in Danzig's Radio Orchestra, changed the mood with romantic *Schlagers*, singing: 'The light goes out and Love comes in.' He sang the last verse with outstretched arms and closed eyes, 'The way into your heart dear, I'll find without a light.' Erich's improved version of this, 'The way into your knickers . . .', was definitely preferable.

And so love came into the house, as the men began to embrace the country girls and they responded. While the older people continued to drink, praising old times and cursing the new ones, the younger guests were groping in earnest, hands going into dresses from above and below.

The Szerszewskis lived on the top floor of a sixteenth-century house. Not many months before, during repairs, a tunnel had been discovered below the cellars. It had revealed the remains of Napoleonic uniforms and weapons, left perhaps by some quartermaster, when Danzig had been a staging-post for the French invasion of Russia. An old mural decorated the walls of the corridor.

Flaking plaster showed a fleet of ships sailing into Danzig harbour on a strong breeze. Doors interrupted the mural. Some of them, usually locked, were open now and straw had been spread on the floors to accommodate visitors for the night. The floor on which they lived had long passages, with unexpected angles, and niches, many small rooms and an attic under the gables.

It had become dark. The older people slumped, open-mouthed, their heads against the wall, or on each others shoulders. The younger ones had mostly disappeared. Bubi, Friedel and I decided to explore. We found some of the guests embracing in passageways, but looking through the keyhole of a bedroom, we were properly rewarded. The dapper German, true to the lyrics he had sung, was in the bed with a Szerszewski niece, a tall, cheerful girl from the outskirts of town. The light was on and though the feather-bedding obscured the details and we had to push one another in grim silence for access to the keyhole, we saw enough to know that this was 'IT'. A formidable task awaited us somewhere in the future and we wanted the details as soon as possible. I did not want to go home that night, but left, fearing my mother's anger.

The following day, on the way to school, I tried to reconstruct what I had seen. There had been great agitation and activity among the feather pillows, but what had been done? I realised that, in the excitement, I had missed important details. Unfortunately, Uncle Fritz's pornographic etchings were too preoccupied with the beauty of shape and movement to bother themselves about the specifics. Nevertheless, I formed a working hypothesis. Some months later in London, my cousin Nils, a year older and with a cosmopolitan *savoir faire*, took me into the privacy of a bathroom and lectured me on the real facts of the matter. His thesis was astonishing. Nils was to devote the rest of his life to this line of research, becoming a gynaecologist. But his theory on that day turned out to be flawed. I had to wait a few years longer and fall into bad company before all was revealed.

The evening after the wake, Bubi, who had been privileged to remain, told me that few guests had been fit to depart. Most had remained, sleeping on the straw-covered floors, the chairs and the toilet. Walking towards the house I saw the last carts and the guests in their crumpled Sunday dresses. Departing, they were barefoot again, heading for the countryside.

Shortly after that, the little musician and the tall niece became engaged. I never saw them again, but one sentence the musician spoke remained in my mind. During an argument with a guest who was critical of the Nazis, he looked about uneasily and said '*Mensch*, keep your mouth shut, or you'll end up as smoke in the chimney.' He must have learnt something in Germany that the people of Danzig still had to be taught.

One afternoon Bubi and I walked down the 'Long Street' which ended at the Motlau River. A dredger was bringing up huge quantities of mud, together with ancient artifacts, and we wanted to watch the work. In the middle of the street, Nazi Stormtroopers had blocked the way with two wooden arches. One was captioned 'For Aryans', the other 'For Jews'. A crowd of grinning people stood about, waiting for a Jew they could trap and beat up.

The Nazis and I had grown up together. When I was a small child, they made their appearance as marginal street louts. As I grew older, they were capturing the levers of power and now they were the government of Danzig. I remember no time in my life without them and had therefore taken them for granted. At the age of eleven I was

79

about to have my first direct confrontation. I felt that this mob was expecting me.

I stood in shock, terrified to run that gauntlet, but also unable to go through the Aryan arch. I felt physical fear and humiliation of being rejected as an alien by the community I belonged to, the people of my town. As we came close Bubi grabbed my arm, turned me towards a shop window and whispered, '*Mensch sei doch nicht blöd!*' (Don't be stupid man!). For him it was common sense, or Kashubian wisdom, to evade what could not be confronted. He walked me back to where we had come from, past Toscani, the Italian ice cream parlour. He stopped to buy large ice creams and, exceptionally, paid for us both.

The memory of that day would remain with me. When I came to live in Israel, it was that arch I passed through.

Mr Szerszewski's brother owned the family farm in Kashubia. For three summer holidays I received permission from my mother to join the Szerszewski children for a week or two, to help with the harvest.

The farm consisted of a two-storey house, flanked by stables, a barn, hayloft and outhouses. These surrounded a large farmyard. The front was enclosed by a solid wooden fence with a central gate. The Szerszewski children and I shared an upstairs room with straw-filled beds and feather quilts. The farmer and his wife had sons of working age. A grandmother and two old aunts dealt with the poultry. Harvest time also brought a group of itinerant field-hands, men and women, from the Ukraine, who wore embroidered clothes and worked barefoot. It was part of my task to bring food to them in the fields. They sang sad melodies in beautiful harmony; one man would begin and be joined by a chorus of high-pitched women, who would be balanced in turn by other deep male voices, soaring over the fields. The songs were about girls seeking true love among the fickle country boys, and of men killed in battle, still mourned by the aged women who once were their brides.

The Ukrainians slept together in the great hayloft. Two large dogs, who spent the day in kennels, had their chains lengthened to span the whole courtyard at night and discourage foxes, thieves and ghosts. They barked for much of the night, perhaps because of the Ukrainians or because they sensed the ghosts we could not see.

Our days consisted of exciting chores. Apart from carrying lunch and water to the fields, we would bind and stack the scythed wheat, herd cows and cut peat, relieving the farmer's children for more important work. Sometimes Bubi and I were sent off to ride on heavy carthorses to an inn on the way to Karthaus, to bring back supplies of liquor. It was for the farmer, who was a great consumer, and for the field-hands whose terms of work included vodka at night.

Scything and binding in the fields had other excitements. Two rows of scythers would advance from opposite directions. By the time they confronted each other before a short stretch of uncut wheat, all the hares, snakes, lizards and assorted life was hidden there. The creatures would break out and the women would scream, trying to keep their bare feet in the air, while the men threw themselves on hares and flailed at snakes. The sky was bright and the sun shone, though occasional storm clouds came with thunder and lightning. It was the grandmother's task then to bring out bottles of holy water, spraying the house, the barn, the pigs in the yard and us, chanting prayers for safety from lightning bolts and fire.

Meanwhile, Bubi had fallen in love with one of the Ukrainians, a girl called Marushka. She had a fine, firm

figure, beautiful bare feet and a round, smiling face
framed by her white kerchief. Marushka flirted with her
eyes and laughed at Bubi, who took to calling out her
name in his sleep. They had no common language and it
seemed like a theme for another sad song. In an act of
daring, Bubi persuaded me to spend a night at the top of
the barn with the Ukrainians. They accepted us amicably.
After the vodka had been passed around and we had
drunk our share in manly fashion, the barn began to spin,
voices receded and waves seemed to crash from side to
side in our skulls. We vomited into the straw, heard distant
laughter, slept fitfully and awoke to vomit again. It was a
terrible night, followed by a painful day. Bubi had failed
the test and so had I. After that, Marushka's eyes no longer
flirted with Bubi and when she laughed in the fields, it was
together with a high-pitched chorus of women and the
joke was on us.

I was to see the Ukrainians again in large groups, on the
quay in the Port of Gdynia. They had arrived from the east
in a great migration and waited to embark ships bound for
Chicago. We were there to take leave of friends emigrating
to America. The Ukrainians sat patiently on baskets and
feather bedding and I heard them sing once more. 'At least
they know where they are going,' my mother said as we
stepped over their bundles. There were tears in her eyes,
and I remember that the ground I stood on seemed to
collapse.

In the farmer's house, late in the evening, after a supper
of potato mash and pork rind eaten from a common bowl,
the old women would sit near the fire and tell ghost stories
in Kashubian. Most of them dealt with a castle, built long
ago, which stood where there was now a great bog in the
forest. I had visited it in the safety of daytime and watched
the bubbles of rotting vegetation rise from the green mud.

Much could lie hidden below and the farmer's sons said that heathen objects of wood sometimes came up to the surface after heavy rain. Once, learned men from a university had come to work there for a summer. According to the stories, the castle had disappeared into the bog when the lord who inhabited it refused to leave his pagan ways and accept Christianity. On nights when the moon was full, the lord and his courtiers rose up from the lake, minstrels played and figures walked weeping between the trees, remembering lost splendour. The ghosts, it seemed, were not threatening, only sad. But it was good to be safely under a guilt and to fall asleep with the dogs barking to keep their spirits away.

Once a week, the farmer drove out to the inns of Karthaus to drink himself into oblivion. In the late evening, his horse, which knew its way home unaided, would reappear with the cart, in which the farmer lay sprawled in a drunken stupor. If he continued to sleep, his family could carry him to bed and he would be up again the following morning as if nothing had happened. But if he woke, it was as a dangerous drunk, stumbling around the farmyard, lashing his horsewhip at pigs, poultry and all comers, in a rage that ended in collapse. Perhaps his drinking bouts, sudden rages and the casual brutality with which he and all the other farmers treated their livestock, was a protest against their fate. Life was hard, in a routine of unending work. He was not regarded as a bad man by his family, nor by the farmhands, and he was generally kind and patient with us, the clumsy children from the 'big city'.

Some afternoons I would walk alone into the hilly forest with a basket, to pick wild strawberries, blackberries or mushrooms. A dachshund called Lalka always joined me. I had been warned to beware of snakes among the mushrooms, as well as of boars who could attack one at breeding time, when the only escape lay in climbing a tree. The forest had a smell both pungent and damp. A secondary forest of ferns grew thick between the trees. I learned to find the patches of wild strawberries and to distinguish between poisonous and edible mushrooms. There were few paths. I walked into the dense forest, recognising north by the moss on the tree barks. The cracking of branches and sudden sounds were usually foxes and wolves, the latter harmless in summer. Sometimes a deer would suddenly appear, elegantly framed by the trees. Although I was afraid of the ghosts which the old aunts described, the forest seemed to hold no supernatural dangers, only real ones.

One day, while bending down to pick some strawberries, Lalka and I were attacked by a viper. It shot out, fell between us, and undecided whom to bite, slithered away. We would not have returned to the farm alive had either of us been bitten. I have never felt at ease in the reptile house of a zoo; perhaps that viper was the reason.

Encounters with wood-cutters or women gathering mushrooms would demand the precise greeting, 'Praised be Jesus Christ' and the response, 'In all eternity, Amen.' With some qualms, I limited myself to 'Praised be . . .', leaving the remainder suspended in the air.

On one of my walks along a dirt track deep in the forest, I heard the sound of approaching wheels. I was overtaken by a group of brightly-painted carts, with horses at the front and more tied to the rear. It was a gypsy caravan. I had seen gypsies in the farmyard, the women grabbing at hands to read fortunes, while the men bartered horses. They had coloured handkerchiefs around their necks and quick, dark eyes that looked about for useful details. With Bubi I had once seen the men wearing hairnets roasting potatoes in a field. The horses stood to one side, while two chained bears growled on the other. Bubi whispered that the cooking-pot on the fire had disappeared from the farmhouse that day. His aunt was still looking for it. I was very scared now, as I had heard from the old aunts at the farm that gypsies also kidnapped children, to sell or to turn into gypsies. I hoped that they would pass me by, but the caravan stopped. Men with brown faces and black moustaches looked down at me and dark women peered through the windows of the closed carts. There was a silence that spread ominously. At last the lead driver asked '*Papierosa?*' (cigarette?) and put his finger to his mouth. I shook my head. I was nine years old and didn't smoke. The man clicked his tongue in disgust, flicked his whip and the caravan creaked on. Relief flooded through me; I was not meant to be a gypsy after all.

In the last year of our harvest holidays, a Polish infantry unit held manoeuvres in the forest. It was the year before a war which everyone expected, and Kashubia was the obvious place for an early clash between the Polish and German armies. The infantry unit established its head-quarters in the barn and moved huge food vats, affection-ately called 'Goulash Cannons', into the farmyard. Urgent messengers ran to and fro between the forest and the barn, in which elegant officers sat around maps, held long cigarette-holders between thumb and forefinger and jig-gled their spurs. Dashing cloaks were draped over their shoulders, their uniforms trimmed with silver braid. Their square-topped military hats had visors, framed in silver, mounted with an eagle.

In addition to their formal mode of address, equivalent to the French '*vous*' and the informal '*tu*', the officers used the third person singular when addressing inferiors. 'Let him beware!' we heard an officer bark at his crest-fallen orderly, 'that he may not regret it!' Bubi and I were impressed and tried to imitate their panache. Walking in a stiff strut, with improvised cigarette-holders and cardboard monocles, we addressed the pigs we fed in the third person.

In the forest, I watched soldiers sleep, wash, swear, relieve themselves and bind their feet with long cloth ribbons, the substitute for socks in the Polish army. They looked drab in comparison with the officers on the farm. My Polish was fluent enough by now to speak to them and interpret for Bubi. They let us play with their swords and wear their four-cornered military hats. In exchange we ran their errands, bringing herring and vodka, so the nights would be less depressing in the damp, chilly forest. Sergeant Cyprik was the man who took charge of the vodka. He was a veteran of the French Foreign Legion. He appeared old to us, not so much in years, but in knowledge of the ways of the world and it showed in his eyes. A scar ran down from one ear almost to his lips, like an extra mouth that smiled. We would come to watch when he and his men washed in a forest brook at the end of the day. Sergeant Cyprik's body was a pattern of scars and tattoos which showed exotic figures and named the women he had loved in African brothels. One said 'Oh Mireille!' as if she had meant more to him than all the others. According to the soldiers, he lived mainly on vodka, but was never drunk. In a mellow mood, knowing what we really loved to see, he would whistle a sad, haunting Arab melody and move the muscles of his arm so that the veiled woman tattooed there began to dance, swaying her buttock and head to the rhythm. Bubi and I watched and dreamt of the Foreign Legion, for whom exotic women, one called Mireille, danced at sunset in a desert, far away from Kashubia.

A wonderful smell of pork and pea soup came out of the

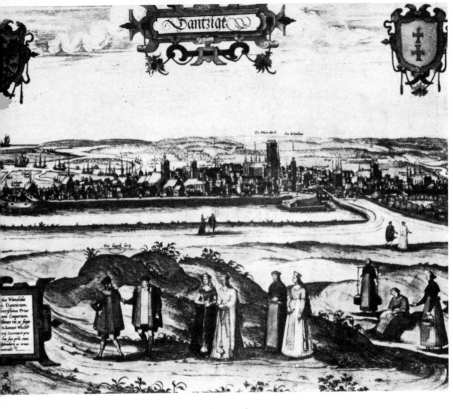

Danzig in the sixteenth century

Danzig in the early nineteenth century

Polish landowners and Danzig merchants negotiating grain prices in the
seventeenth century

Danzig before the war

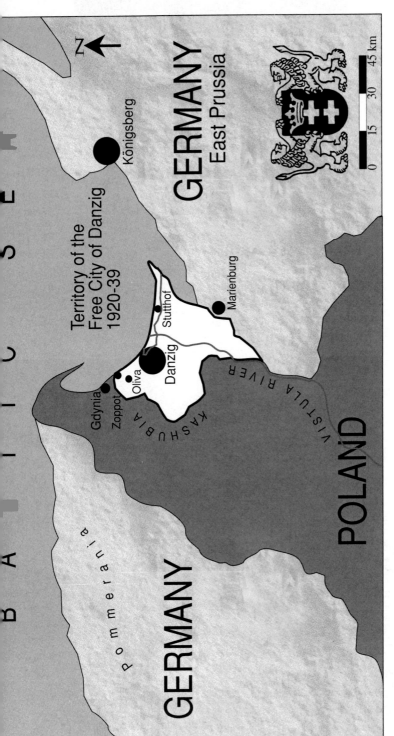

The free city of Danzig and its territory, 1920–1939, as drawn by the author

A child's-eye view of marching Nazis

Albert Forster, Hitler's *Gauleiter* in Danzig (*Photograph courtesy of the Wiener Library, London*)

Louis Boss

Franz Boss mounted on Max, Flanders, 1917

My mother *(centre)* with Ruth and Kurt Regan in the 1920s

My father at the Russian high school in Lomza

Franz and Lucie Boss and my mother in Wiesbaden

'Ratz-Batz' Arthur Levandovsky as a Death's-Head Hussar

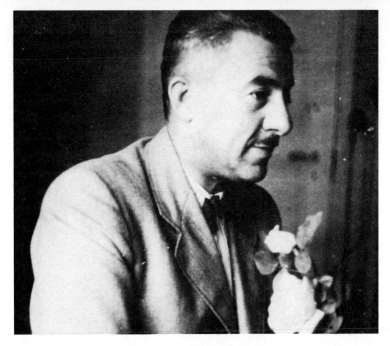

Uncle Fimek and Mr Gold

At the *Volksschule (middle row, second left)*. 'Uncle' Peter is on my left

cooking vats at lunchtime and in the evenings. We lined up with the soldiers and received our share. The officers flirted with the beautiful farmer's niece who had come on a visit from Torun and whose face shone like the sun, as well as a cousin from the USA who had arrived with her. The cousin was the first American I had ever seen. She was a well-mannered Polish girl from Chicago, with curlers in her hair, who crossed herself each time I swore. I therefore made sure that she did it often. In exchange, she taught me the foxtrot. We danced on the fern-covered forest floor. She led, turning me about while I whistled the latest *Schlager* I had picked up in Danzig: 'Erika, Erika, do you need a friend who sends red roses in the daytime and is honest in intent?' Perhaps the girls were the real reason for the headquarter's location in the farmyard – if not for the manoeuvres themselves. The American cousin, her curlers protected by a silk scarf, kissed me warmly on the mouth when she joined Lalka and me on forest walks. I hope that the officers were at least as lucky.

The year was 1938. I never returned, because I would leave Danzig the following summer. The events that followed would obliterate my memory of those times spent in Kashubia. After the war I tried to trace Bubi but without success. He was certainly conscripted into the German army and probably killed. I wish that I could have thanked him for the good times we had together.

In 1989 I revisited Danzig for the first time since my childhood. A friend had persuaded me to make the trip with him. While there we decided to register for a day-tour into the Kashubian countryside. Following directions, we found our official Polish travel guide in a little office. He introduced himself as Franek and sized up his customers.

Did we want to buy a German map of Danzig? It appeared from under the table, expensive and illegal, because as history was now taught in Poland, this had always been a Polish city. On the wall of Franek's office, next to posters of the Mazurian lakes, hung pictures of nudes in thought-provoking poses. A camp-bed had been tucked into a corner – I wondered at its purpose. We bought tickets for a tour that would leave on the following day.

With the German map we were able, at last, to identify the original street names and piece together the little that remained of the places I remembered. For two days, we searched for the city that I had left fifty years ago. The Polish street names and massive wartime destruction made our task difficult. Danzig had been bombed into rubble half a century ago, but the shell-holes in the roofs and walls of abandoned houses seemed to make the passage of time irrelevant. Whatever had been erected since the war was dull or grey. Where the accidental survival of original buildings awoke a memory, it vanished before the next row of concrete blocks. The war memorial on the old Wood-Market had been replaced by a Polish monument. The houses surrounding the market square had disappeared and with it the window from which Annie Kirsch had looked down on the riot, while I had looked at her.

A part of the waterfront and much of the historic Langgasse had their façades reconstructed. It resembled an open-air museum or a film set on the lot of a Hollywood studio. And yet, it was enough to confirm that this had once been among the most beautiful streets in Europe. As my mother and I had last lived in a corner house off that street, I looked for our entrance. There was no doorway. The 'Long-Street' had been reconstructed from seventeenth-century drawings and etchings. Side views had apparently not been available, and had I found a door it would, in any case, have led nowhere. Postwar Danzig, now Gdansk, is another place. A child will continue to walk through the streets and alleys of an adult's memory.

The residents of the city were newcomers. They had escaped from the farmlands of eastern Poland, when the Russian army annexed that territory, and had no roots in Danzig, only squatter's rights. The passengers with whom we shared the bus to Kashubia were elderly Germans and their families, brought back by nostalgia for one more glimpse of the region they had been expelled from in 1944.

Franek, whose German included an extensive repertoire of laboured jokes, explained the Kashubians through his microphone as though we were about to visit a home of the mentally-retarded. There was an amused understanding between him and the German tourists that the Kashubians were more than a little dull. In mitigation, he acknowledged the name of one general in the distant past who had been a Kashubian. Beyond that, apparently nothing of note since the dawn of history.

We passed through the countryside of farmland and lakes, familiar to me from my childhood. In Karthaus, a four-man orchestra awaited us. Their performance seemed designed to confirm the opinion of our guide and his tourists. The band was dressed in a nondescript national costume, coloured ribbons hanging from their hats. Among the instruments was a stick with bells that tinkled when hit against the ground; it recalled the caps worn by mediæval fools. The orchestra sang the national anthem of Kashubia in their dialect, to the amusement of the tourists. I began to suspect that this pathetic show could be a joke played at our expense, rather than the other way round. The war, after all, had swept over the

Kashubs, as it had so many times in the past and they had bent their heads to let it pass. The war destroyed Poland and Germany, but the Kashubs continued to farm and to fish. It seemed to me that this might be a gift worth more than any number of obscure generals and forgotten statesmen. Perhaps the Kashubians had perfected the art of survival in difficult terrain and it consisted of being so unremarkable that nobody noticed.

I looked past an expanse of fields towards a hilly forest and remembered that the farmhouse lay there. I knew that a wooden tower stood at the top of the hill, visible above the tall trees and that its name was *Wiezyca*. I could have found my way back and, skirting a small lake, encountered the path that led to the farmhouse. There, during the manoeuvres, two soldiers, sword in hand, had stood guard, surrounded by grazing cows. The grass that came up to my knees when I ran there last, would now reach the top of my shoes. I was afraid that whatever else I might encounter would likewise have shrunk, when measured with the cool eye of an adult. I was relieved that our tour schedule left me no time for such exploration. I suppose that the grandson of the farmer would now be ploughing that land and that the dogs still bark, to fend off foxes, thieves and ghosts in the night.

Little Poland in Petershagen

WHEN THE NAZIS governing Danzig banned Jewish children from all schools, the Jewish community organised its own school system, a primary and a high school. It was staffed by teachers also expelled from all institutions of learning, who served the diminishing community until its destruction in 1940. My cousins, including 'uncle' Peter and friends, began to attend the newly founded school, the Dr Rosenbaum Gymnasium, which was efficient and set high standards.

My parents then decided on another course for me. I would enter the Polish High School in Danzig. It was my father's wish that I should learn French and in time attend the French Lycée in Warsaw, which would then allow me to go to a university in France. The Polish High School was to be the stepping stone in that direction and France my final destination. Although it could not be fully realised, this plan was to have far-reaching repercussions in my life.

My father, an admirer of all things French, spoke the language well and loved French literature. He recited long passages of French poetry to me '. . . for the sake of the melody and the rhythm.' The book I saw him reading when we parted in Warsaw, was Yolande Foldes' *La Rue du chat qui pêche*. It was the story of Hungarian refugees in this, the smallest street in Paris. Years later, on my first visit and in my father's memory, I searched and found that little street of four houses near the Quai St Michel.

Unfortunately, my father also believed in France's military might: its army and weapons outnumbered those of the Germans and its defense system, the Maginot Line, was invincible. He took the French at their word, failing to distinguish between the beauty of French rhetoric and the impotence it disguised. It sounded very convincing to hear him predict that France would defeat Nazi Germany decisively if a war broke out. My departure for England was mainly due to pressure on my mother by her sisters in London, who were in a position there to see the events and dangers more clearly. To my father it was no more than a prudent interruption of the schooling he had planned for me. But reality intervened. Within six weeks of Hitler's order to invade France, an operation which he graced with the codename 'Danzig', France had collapsed like a soufflé. By that time, however, it was too late for my father to reassess the situation. He and my mother were on their way to the death camps. In our family, my father was the last Francophile.

The rights granted to Poland in the Free City of Danzig by the Treaty of Versailles, a post office, rail and harbour facilities amongst them, also included the establishment of a Polish High School. It was an impressive showpiece, designed primarily as a political act. The school was a large, modern building, near the town centre in Petershagen. It was close to a railway station of the same name, for trains bound to and from Poland. To attend the Polish High School, I had first to learn the language. During my last year at the *Volksschule*, a teacher came to the house in the evenings to teach me Polish. He was a very serious boy called Tomasz, himself a recent graduate from that high school. As his ambition was to be an airforce pilot my first lessons were in aeronautics. The first Polish word he taught me was '*samolot*' (self-flyer/ airplane). After that came the hymn of the Polish airforce: 'Winged flyer, master of the boundless world, disdaining death, life smiling from your face . . .' Poland's airforce was small and had the panache of a cavalry in the air. Tomasz's need to be among them might have stemmed from the ambivalence of having a Jewish mother who had converted to marry a Pole. He attained his goal. Sadly, he was killed within hours of the outbreak of war.

It was not easy for me to learn Polish. As a Slavic language, it bears no similarity to German, the only language I spoke. It has a complex grammar of seven declensions and is heavily committed to the sounds railway engines make, sc, rzcz, z and szcz, pronounced in rapid succession and with few vowels. With the word for a beetle spelled *chszaszcz*, the language was a tongue-twister for a novice. 'I don't want Polish, it's French I want to learn,' I complained to my father, on a visit to Gdynia. We had been to the cinema and seen *La Grande Illusion*; Jean Gabin, with his nonchalance, a cigarette hanging from his lower lip, seemed to me the embodiment of manliness and I wanted to sound like him. 'Later,' my father said, 'that will come later.' But it never did.

The day came when I had to take the entrance examination. I sat in a spacious classroom, well lit, with large windows, in rows with other, mostly Polish, children. The atmosphere was very different from the Neo-Gothic gloom of my previous school. I remember the intense embarrassment of only half-understanding the language in which the papers were written. During the oral interview, I stumbled over the complex pronunciation, confused the seven declensions and noted the amused smiles of the examiners. I went home in a black mood, feeling that I had made a fool of myself and failed. Some weeks later, to

93

my surprise, the notice came that I had passed. Mr Tomasz had either done a better job than I had realised, or the school was very keen to attract more pupils.

The Polish High School was well staffed and had excellent facilities. There were not, however, enough Polish-speaking pupils in Danzig to fill it. Its convenient location, next to a railway station, meant that many of the pupils, as well as the staff, could be imported from Poland to Danzig every morning by train and sent back across the border every afternoon. This was a nice piece of political engineering, as it justified the school academically, while adding a few hundred Poles to Danzig, at least during daytime. As a Danzig institution, the school was therefore part fact, part fiction.

The school I now walked to every day was an ambivalent experience for me. Here was a different language and culture and a wider curriculum than I had been prepared for. Caning too was now a thing of the past. It was co-educational and therefore full of exciting possibilities. And yet I walked that route each morning with reluctance, past the rusticated walls of the High Gate, the monument of the Kaiser on his prancing horse, and the Central Synagogue, to pass through a doorway and enter a country that was alien and hostile.

Unfortunately, that culture included an aspect I had not encountered before: anti-Semitism, Polish-style. Much has been written on the subject. For me, it tainted the entire period I spent at the school and my reaction to Poles ever since. Nazi-controlled though the German schools were, it is a curious, no doubt accidental, fact that I experienced no racial encounter with those pupils or teachers. At the outset, German anti-Semitism was decreed from above and as the Germans obey their orders, that order too was followed with varying degrees of relish or reluctance.

Although the pupils and teachers regularly appeared in Nazi uniforms, I remember no incidents directed against Jewish classmates. When, on one sensitive occasion, we were told to draw a trumpet with a Nazi banner attached to it, we tentatively explained to the teacher that it was not a suitable subject for Jewish children. He agreed, and while the rest of the class drew the trumpet with the banner, ours was without.

To the Jewish adults, the anti-Semitic legislation, the physical danger and economic ruin, must have been terrifying. But a child's view is limited to his own imme-diate field of vision. All the shops in Danzig carried signs banning Jews from entering. The polite ones were worded 'Jews not desired', cruder ones read, 'Entry strictly for-bidden to dogs and Jews'. In the acrobatics of daily sur-vival, the shops in which Jews were merely 'not desired' came to sound, in time, as though they were extending a gracious invitation. Jews were banned from all public places, including cafés and cinemas. Alone or with friends, I do not remember that I paid much attention to any of this and filtered through those terrors practically invisible to the system and almost oblivious of it.

Polish anti-Semitism, on the other hand, rose up from below, rooted in centuries of religious hatred and economic antagonism. Jews had been imported into Poland in mediæval times. Polish society, consisting of a small land-owning aristocracy, the '*Szlachta*', and a mass of unemancipated serfs, had not produced a trading-class similar to the mercantile economies of the West. Polish kings gave incentives to Jews to enter their lands and assume that role. Wedged between the two existing orders, Jews were seen as economic exploiters, alien intruders and sinister Christ-killers.

The history of the Jews in Poland is a sad and weary

pattern of permanent hostility and murderous pogroms. The last recorded pogrom occurred in postwar Poland in 1946, killing some of the few survivors not exterminated by the Germans. Between the two world wars, the Jews comprised about three million of Poland's thirty million inhabitants. By the end of World War II less than fifty thousand Jews survived.

In the decades preceding the Second World War, the Polish intelligentsia adopted fascism as a modern ideology, suiting their ancient anti-Semitic prejudices. To the masses, it was ordained by the Church. To the Polish Government, the 'Jewish Problem' was useful in deflecting attention from their own incompetence. It took no action against pogroms organised by the right-wing parties, connived at anti-Jewish boycotts and the withholding of bank credits to Jewish enterprises. At all levels, hostility to Jews was a national preoccupation. The Jewish reaction varied: attempts to blend into Polish culture among a section of intellectuals, often including conversion; a banding together of the majority ghetto-style or emigration to the West and Palestine. Access to higher education for Jewish students was restricted. For those who succeeded, life was made difficult by Polish Nationalist and Fascist student organisations. At many universities, including those of Warsaw and Lodz, Jewish students were forced to sit on separate benches or attend lectures standing up.

This was the phenomenon which crossed the Polish border each morning to Petershagen and departed in the evening. During the day, together with other Jewish pupils, I had to face it. Most Jewish children at the school were recent arrivals in Danzig. Their fathers were businessmen involved in commerce between Danzig and Poland, and they seemed more conditioned to regard this hostility as a facet of everyday life. Unprepared for it, I was outraged. Before long I was pushed, kicked and called a 'dirty *zyd*'. My response was to be aggressive in return, quick to fight in the classroom, on the stairs and in the playground. I found that, unlike German and English children, who stand aside during a fight between two boys, Polish children joined in to kick the combatant not to their liking. I had to fight often and hard, as I had already learned in the streets of Danzig and among the competing leech collectors on the Motlau.

I had also absorbed Danzig's anti-Polish prejudices. Regarded as dim-witted and primitive, Poles were the butt of local jokes and street-songs. If anyone was 'inferior', it was certainly not me! Goaded by indignities, I defended myself. Matters came to a climax when I brought a Swiss army knife into class. A present from my father, it included scissors, a corkscrew and a pebble-remover for horses' hooves. While I showed off these virtues, one of the bullies, a broad, fat-faced boy called Pawel, pulled it from my hand, saying: 'I'll keep it, it's too good for a Jew!' I grabbed it back after a short scuffle and shouted 'the only way you'll get it is stuck up your arse.' 'I'll teach you a lesson, *zyd*!' said Pawel and rushed off with two friends to the teacher's office to report that I had threatened him at knife-point. His friends corroborated the story. Professor Urbanek, who taught English, practised sang-froid and smoked an English pipe, was not an excitable man, but the idea of boys fighting with knives in his class made him very indignant. He never asked me for an explanation. I was unhappily surprised, some days later, to see my mother descending the school stairs, after a heavy interview with the professor, as I came up from the schoolyard. My expulsion seemed likely. 'What will your father say when he hears of this in Warsaw?'

That evening, my mother and I had a great row which

97

ended in tears on her side and sullen silence on mine. Curiously, I never told her what I was going through at school. I would have told my father, but I felt that a woman should not be involved. In German, the gap is great between the words *Männersachen* and *Frauensachen* – the concerns of men and those of women. Fortunately Professor Urbanek and his council of teachers relented. I was to be on probation, not expelled.

The incident became a turning point for the better. The rumour of Pawel's complaint circulated around the playground; I was now a knife-wielding tough. The hustling stopped and the bullies regarded me with some respect. I had become one of them. Other boys also sidled up to pay their ultimate compliment: 'Pity you're a Jew.' As most of my classmates returned to Poland each afternoon, I saw little of them outside school. My evenings were spent in the company of my cousins and friends I had made before.

During my mother's visits to my father in Poland, I stayed with my 'Uncle' Peter and his family on the 'Elizabeth Moat'. My grandfather's brother, Georg, and his wife, had four children. Peter was the youngest. I spent hours on the floor with him, drawing with crayons on brown wrapping paper what we imagined life to be behind the façades of Danzig's houses. Rats and old newspapers held sway in the attic. Skeletons moulded in the basements and tunnels beneath the city. On the other floors, people ate, laughed, fought, made love and died. I drew the buildings I passed daily, the 'Stock-tower', with cells and torture chambers and the Arsenal with the grim, stone warrior who stood on a severed head outside the gate. We drew passionately and quickly, inventing our own hieroglyphics to capture it all.

We also included the life of our upstairs neighbour, Gauleiter Albert Forster, Hitler's man in Danzig. We knew that he was on the telephone to the Führer daily, assuring him of Danzig's absolute loyalty and complaining about his great rival, Greisser, the Nazi president of the Danzig parliament. Hitler would apparently respond graciously to the fawning and be evasive about the complaints. He liked the two to spy on one another and keep him informed. We drew their bubbles of conversation which, I learned later from the diaries of those close to him and Hitler, were quite accurate. Forster, in his smart uniform, was polite to us on the staircase and very courteous to Thea, Georg's wife. 'How is your son, dear lady?' he asked after her oldest boy, Hans, had left on the first illegal transport for Palestine. 'Do let me know!'

The Gauleiter was known for the fortune he had amassed as a result of his corruption. The system offered ample scope for enrichment to entrepreneurs with Swastika armbands. The people called them *Bonzen* (big-wigs) and lamented that the 'dear Führer' didn't know. In fact, the Führer didn't care. Corruption was no hindrance to anyone in the Nazi leadership.

I remember loud-speakers blaring out Forster's speeches through the city, and heard the rousing cheers. Through the windows of the Elizabeth Moat, I watched his organised marches. A sea of flaming torches advanced in the dark, illuminating singing faces: 'With Jews' blood spurting off our knives, things will go twice as well!'

Forster would deliver his last speech six years later, before the Soviet army reached Danzig. He exhorted the citizens to fight: 'Danzig is and remains German – *Heil Hitler!*' Broadcast over the radio, he had prudently pre-recorded it before his own escape by submarine as the city was being shelled into oblivion. The citizens could hear his words at about the time soldiers of the Red Army entered Danzig to rape and loot what remained. They could savour them as the male population was paraded down the Hindenburg Boulevard on their way to forced labour in the Soviet Union, from which few returned. According to witnesses this was the moment when the people of Danzig suddenly remembered that they were not Germans after all, but victims of a great error. They were a little late. Danzig had just been annexed by Poland, renamed Gdansk, and everyone in it would shortly be expelled.

The British Army caught Forster, delivered him to the Poles and he was sentenced to death. His rival Greisser was also caught and paraded through town in a cage before his execution. Both were responsible for Danzig's destruction and mass murder. They deserved their fate.

Eva was my only friend at the Polish High School. She was a lock-keeper's daughter from along the river and walked home in my direction. Her parents were Kashubians. We spoke German as soon as we were out of the school as her Polish was no better than mine. We often met on the way to school and returned together, walking along the Reitbahn, Langgasse and beyond. I had to walk fast to keep up with Eva's long legs, encased in woollen stockings. Her plaits were blonde, her eyes blue and she wore the school cap at a rakish angle. In Danzig, it would have been reckless bravery for a boy to wear that cap, or any other insignia of the Polish High School; one got beaten up for it by children in the street. My own cap was usually folded inside my shirt, giving it a broken look. That way one distinguished the pupils who lived in Danzig from those who returned to Poland with their caps uncreased.

On our way home, we walked through the monumental gate that led into the Langgasse and looked at the papers displayed on its walls. I liked the *Stürmer* best. It was the Nazis' official anti-Semitic newspaper, edited in Berlin by

Julius Streicher. It sweated with hate. There were drawings of grotesque monsters with fat bodies, black hats and
large noses who sat in spiders'-webs of intrigue, guarded
money-bags, directed world Communism and in their
spare time violated blonde women. I liked those monsters,
as they were obviously smarter and had more fun than the
square-headed blonde giants who hated them so hysterically.

One day, at the peak of a heatwave, the senior boys of
the school ran into the playground and, chanting in
chorus, demanded the day off. The school principal, Mr
Augustinski, bowed to popular demand. School was over
by lunchtime. 'If we run,' said Eva, 'we can get to a wedding where I know the bride.' I followed her to a church,
but we were too late. The last guests had left. Only Leo
remained, open-mouthed, examining the money in his
gloved hand. Everyone knew him. As always, he was
dressed in tuxedo and top hat. His body was bent and he
shuffled as he walked. Though his clothes were thread-
bare, Leo was the best-dressed man in town. One gloved
hand kept church and synagogue doors open, while he
collected alms with the other. I had seen him all my life,
but never stood so close to him before. Sometimes I saw him
on a passing hearse, next to the coachman, his appearance
adding solemnity to the occasion. As a small child, I hid
whenever I saw him, taking him for Danzig's Public
Executioner. We all knew that the executioner performed
his decapitations dressed in a tuxedo and white gloves and
I assumed that he walked about choosing his victims at
random. Leo shuffled off and the church door closed.

Eva and I walked through the St John's Gate to the river
and bought ice cream. We cadged a handful of small fish
from the Kashubian fishwives at the market, who would as
soon oblige you as hit you with a flounder. Walking

towards the amber shops, along the quay, Eva threw the fish into the air to shrieking seagulls. We looked at necklaces and brooches and the lumps of amber with spiders and beetles embedded in them. In one of the amber pieces, a spider and a fly lay together, the rolling sap had permanently united the diner and his meal.

A detachment of Nazis came marching down the narrow quay in twos. One hand on their belt-buckles, the other swung stiffly, boots beating on the cobbled stones. Their commander owned the sausage shop my mother sent me to. Shop assistants and clerks, round-shouldered and potbellied, sang: 'Brown-black is the hazelnut, I am brownblack too. Brown-black shall my sweetheart be, just as I am too!' They were heroes marching towards a new World Order.

I looked at Eva. She was still facing the shop window. After a silence she said, 'We are all flies in amber, each stuck in his own lump.' Her eyes were wet. I stroked her arm, alarmed at the tears as well as the concept. My mother was in the habit of turning life into black epigrams. Here was a new source. We held hands and for the first time, I walked her home. We made plans to take the tram to the beach at Heubude the following Sunday, where the sands contained rough pellets of amber and small fish with razor-sharp fins swam close to the shore; but we never went. Was she my girlfriend? Just as with everything else about our lives, I was uncertain.

Education now had me in its grip. A burly teacher taught ancient history. Enraged by wrong answers, he threw chalk at us, bellowing like a bull while the creases on his bald head formed an awesome triangle. We called him 'Apis', after the sacred bull of Egypt. He taught us the Laws of Hammurabi and the ways of the Pharaohs. With his chalk ever ready and his aim accurate from decades of practice, it was remarkable how quickly we learned long passages of *The Odyssey*. What they lacked in pathos was made up for by their speed. English was taught by Professor Urbanek. 'See-saw up and see-saw down, the sky is blue and the ground is brown', was the first verse we learned. It was wise, as well as being English, and I remember it every time I aim for the blue sky and hit the brown ground instead.

Thanks to Erich who tutored me, I was good at Latin. As my Polish was still weak, my mother arranged for an occasional helper. Ida was a dark, Polish-Jewish girl, a recent arrival in Danzig. About twenty-four years old, she lived in Jacob's Lane with her widowed father and younger sister. The girls worked as seamstresses. Their father, a good-natured, religious man, walked about the house in a much worn suit and hat. The girls looked demure, with long sleeves and skirts down to their shoes. Their small flat smelt of boiled fish. As soon as the father left, homework was interrupted. They jumped up in excitement, put money into my hand and sent me off to the nearest pork-butcher for sliced ham. It had to be consumed quickly, in case Papa returned. I liked them for being so nicely wicked behind a pious façade. They were also romantic and with their father out of the way introduced me to the verses of Juljan Tuvim, a`Polish poet I have liked ever since:

'I hear your heart's blood beat in your white breast,
And live by blind love in this life so full of death.'

The girls, who had acted in a Yiddish amateur theatre in their home town, danced while they recited it in tango rhythm. I can still hear their voices. Thanks to them, my

103

Polish improved.

We had two art teachers at the school. Professor Szyszko-Bogusz was a man in a state of permanent enthusiasm and the peak of his joy was to see us paint distorted reality. Human figures were expected to have double noses, blue faces and a forest of fingers on each hand. It confirmed his theory that children's painting was natural and fresh, if uncorrupted by adult influences. We were already corrupt however, and knew from older boys that the way to good marks was to manufacture the spontaneity he wanted. I raided Uncle Fritz's art books for ideas from Otto Dix, Picasso and Grosz. As he was producing a book on the spontaneity of children's art, the professor was delighted with us. Our drawings were sent off to his publishers in Warsaw.

By contrast, Mr Wendrowski, the school's other art teacher, demanded realism. 'The secret lies in the shadows,' was his cryptic instruction, as we sketched in the park near the school. We tried to unravel that secret with thick black pencils. If one drew the shadow of a tree with its foliage, would the remaining area reveal the tree? I experimented and took the riddle with me into later life.

The teachers were generally indifferent to the anti-Semitic behaviour of the pupils and while they did not participate, neither did they combat it. It was, after all, part of Polish life. Only Professor Pastwa, who taught geography, enjoyed it. 'Don't try to make me feel sorry,' he said, smiling to a Jewish girl, crippled by polio, as she limped up to the drawing-board, 'your sort all have rich fathers.' The class smirked in approval. A rotund man, with pomaded dark hair, he was a member of the Fascist Party and wore its insignia on his lapel. Anti-Semitic asides were part of the entertainment in his lessons. Professor Pastwa and I shared a secret. I had seen him one evening in a doorway in Danzig embracing a boy. We had recognised each other. I was vaguely aware that I had some power over him; he must have been acutely aware of it. My marks in geography were uniformly good. Ten years later, studying Architecture at Manchester University, a Polish student approached me. 'I have regards for you from my uncle. He taught you geography.' It was Professor Pastwa's nephew. 'Where is he now?' I asked. 'He escaped to Romania and lives there.'

In the Air Force, some years before, I had attended a course at which aerial photographs of innocent landscapes were placed before us. We were taught that with concentration and a keen eye it was possible to see tanks hiding in a little wood and artillery disguised as bushes. With this past training, I concentrated hard on Professor Pastwa's message and detected what was hidden beneath the foliage: 'Greetings, Jewish brat, with your lousy Polish, to whom I gave better marks than you deserved, from the homosexual Fascist whose little secret you knew. You and I share a bigger secret now. We are among the few who survived out of those thousands. We two share the triumph of the living and the guilt that comes with it. We shall never meet, but I know that you will never forget me and I will never forget you.'

Once a week we received a religious lesson. While a Catholic priest came to instruct the class, Jewish children were taught religion and Hebrew by a rabbi. It was an hour during which we could play games, throw paper pellets and tease girls. We knew that however ignorant we remained of the Hebrew language and the prophet Samuel, the rabbi was too good-hearted to fail us. Perhaps he did not want to create more problems than we already had.

Physical Education was administered by a wiry man with a grim smile. His favourite exercise was to form a gauntlet of boys, who pelted us with tennis balls as we raced past. 'You're dead! You're dead!' he shouted as the balls hit their target and we winced in pain. It was intended to teach us discipline under fire. On one festive occasion, he introduced a guest athlete, Poland's champion runner, Miss Walasiewiczowna. She had recently distinguished herself at the Berlin Olympic Games. We watched her run at great speed. She was very muscular and the talcum on her face did not disguise her need of a shave. Miss Walasiewiczowna was to make Olympic history again on her recent death. It was discovered that she was, in fact, a man. I am surprised that it took so long to establish the obvious.

In history lessons we learned that Poland, once a strong kingdom, collapsed due mainly to the anarchy of its nobles. Their system of electing kings on the unanimous vote of the aristocracy had given rise to intrigues and bribery by the surrounding powers of Austria, Russia and emerging Prussia. Poland, now weaker than its neighbours, was invaded and partitioned in stages. By the eighteenth century, it had become little more than several provinces of the empires of the three powers. A period of insurrections and brutal repressions followed until the First World War. The final uprisings occurred when the war had brought the three powers to the verge of collapse. By 1920, Poland was restored, within borders determined at the Treaty of Versailles. There was an anecdote, not related at school, of the Polish delegation being received at Versailles by President Wilson. The President said, 'Gentlemen, I am happy to tell you that Poland will exist again, though not quite within the boundaries you demanded.' 'Terrible news!' exclaimed the delegates, 'when we inform our people, there will be demonstrations and riots and there will be pogroms!' President Wilson was distressed and recalled the delegation some days later. 'Gentlemen,' he said, 'I am happy to inform you that Poland will receive its territorial demands in full.' 'Wonderful news!' exclaimed the delegates, 'when we tell this to our people there will be joy and celebrations and there will be pogroms!'

Postwar Poland contained substantial minorities, whom the Poles treated no better than they had themselves been treated by their former occupiers. With a rural economy, little industry, high illiteracy and a tiny intelligentsia, it was governed by military leaders who had fought for independence in past uprisings. The charismatic leader of Poland's independence, Marshal Pilsudski, had just died. His place was taken by the generals and colonels who had been under him. Their portraits were much in evidence at our school and throughout Poland. At music classes, we learned the songs of the insurrections. Their theme was Fatherland and Death. 'Hey Poles! Forward to the Bayonets!' was a song which puzzled us, as we did not understand whether it was an invitation to throw ourselves onto them or to use them in a charge. Fortunately the Polish words for bayonet and females are so similar that sung in chorus they were indistinguishable and made more sense. There were also songs to be learned in praise of the present leaders. 'Marshal Smigly-Rydz, our dear and valiant leader, command us and we will follow!' was the opening line of one. It could not have been easy for the songwriter to find a word that rhymed with Smigly-Rydz. 'We will not yield one button,' was another inspired line. Poland lost all its buttons once the war broke out, despite the bravery of the Polish Army, while the political generals and colonels about whom we sang, disappeared without trace.

The Polish government's policy was to counter German

expansionism by an alliance with France and England. Just as Germany had successfully used its minority in Czechoslovakia as a pretext for invading that country, so it had, for some time, used the 'Danzig Question' against the Poles. This was not difficult. With a German population in the Free City forced by treaty to give Poland trade and port facilities, there were always undercurrents of tension, fuelled now by the Nazis. One example concerned postage stamps. Poland's rights in Danzig included the maintenance of their own post office. In mid-1938 it issued a series of stamps. The Nazis objected to the graphics. One showed Polish grain merchants trading in the city. In response, the Poles pointed out that the picture was a reproduction of a seventeenth-century Dutch painting, which had been hanging in the Danzig Town Hall for the past three centuries. Protests and counter-protests filled diplomatic pouches and newspapers, following on earlier quarrels and preceding new ones, each progressively more virulent. Poland had countered these provocations by constructing a port on its narrow strip of Baltic shoreline next to Danzig. Thanks to French aid, the small fishing village of Gdynia was transformed into a large port. Within a decade it allowed Poland unhindered sea-traffic, no longer at the whim of the Danzig authorities. As a consequence, Danzig suffered a substantial loss of revenue. In compensation, it received subsidies from Berlin and earned them by further provoking the Poles.

And so, while we were learning about it at school, the history of Poland, and much more, was being written on the streets through which we walked.

Anatevka without the Fiddler

D URING THE EASTER HOLIDAYS in 1938, my father asked
me to come to Warsaw and join him on a journey
which, I believe, was meant to show me something of his
youth and Jewish life. I was learning the implications of
being Jewish from the Nazis and the Poles. The meaning
of being Jewish was more difficult to grasp. Among the
earliest stories my father told me was one of a wise rabbi to
whom a stranger came and demanded 'Teach me Judaism
while I stand on one foot!' The rabbi looked at the man's
shaking leg and said, 'Love your neighbour, all the rest is
embellishment.' I learnt the meaning of Judaism standing
on one foot before my father.

I grew up with a repertoire of Yiddish songs which he
must have sung to me when I was very small. It seemed
that I had known them all my life. 'Under the cradle
stands a snow-white goat. Sleep on my child and when
you're a man, raisins and almonds will be your trade.' Now
that I create heavy, metal sculptures and ship them to faraway places, I often regret that I cannot make them out of
raisins.

With my father's songs and stories came a bond of
warmth and intimacy that survived years of separation and
helped me when it was my turn to raise children. Some of
the tales went over my head and I understood them only
in later years:

109

A man with painful haemorrhoids went to a rabbi and complained that his suffering interfered with his learning and prayers. The rabbi put his hand on the man's shoulder and said, 'How do you know which is more pleasing to God, my friend, your prayers or your haemorrhoids?'

I doubt that such a thought would have been allowed to set foot in our synagogue. Attendance there was formal and correct. We entered *en famille*, a social act that gave due acknowledgement to God in the expectation that he would return the compliment. Only my mother refused to attend, claiming that God was Man's creation, not the other way around.

I recall running home after a week at school to announce that I could now spell my name. As I struggled with the first signature of my life, a rain of coins fell on the table. I looked at the ceiling and saw my father smiling above me. Recently I found a children's book, printed a century ago. It depicts a *cheder* (religious class). Diligent children are taught the *Tanach* (Bible) while a rain of coins falls on them from the heavens. My father had gone to *cheder* somewhere in Poland and must have known that image. A moment of pure joy so long ago, and a lifetime before I found its origin.

'Loving one's neighbour is very difficult,' my father said, when I questioned him further about the man with a shaking leg. 'It's enough to remember that he's entitled to love. That makes you a *Mensch*, and being a *Mensch* is more important than being religious.' With that, my father had to leave Danzig and our meetings in Warsaw and across the border were too short and busy for further theology.

The journey with my father was to take us to Lomza. I knew the name because he had gone to High School there.

The Tsar ruled in Russia and Lomza, like most of Poland, was within his Empire. A small child, with thin face and large, dark eyes, my father had worn a black, high-collared uniform, with silver buttons and a double-eagle on his cap. In those times, entrance into High School was severely restricted for Jewish children. In addition to excellent marks at an entrance examination, a substantial bribe and a willing school-inspector had to be found. It seems that my grandfather found this combination in Lomza. Little Mishka was lodged with relatives in the nearby village of Lomzica. At five each morning he marched for miles up the cracked dirt-road, often deep in mud and snow, towards Lomza where he learned mathematics, history and Russian literature. At night he trudged back to a chorus of barking dogs. By the time he graduated, Poland had become independent and the rest of his studies were at university and in Polish, but my father's affection for the Russian language remained. 'French for the intellect, Russian for the soul, German for the bill,' he used to say. So a few Russian songs had also infiltrated my repertoire, 'Black Eyes' and 'The Little Gypsy Girl' among them.

Meanwhile, the relatives in Lomzica had grown old. My father decided to take me to the scene of his youth. After a day in Warsaw, we boarded a train, accompanied by Uncle Fimek, who had his own reasons for the journey. Although the train was crowded, the first-class compartment was empty except for an elderly gentleman who had grey hair that stood high on his head, a fierce, waxed moustache and a large, red nose. A fur rug covered his body and after peering at us with deep disapproval, he burrowed into it and disappeared. To my surprise, another man standing outside the compartment, equally red-nosed and moustached, appeared to be his double. My father had also noticed this oddity and we exchanged glances.

The countryside sped by while we played checkers with Fimek. Perhaps in preparation for his journey into the past, my father began to recite the poems of Pushkin in Russian. 'Listen,' he said, 'how the very sound of these words suggests snow under horses' hooves. And here is a description of an evil woman . . .' Though I understood nothing, I clearly heard the horses' galloping over crunching snow, followed by the hissing and coiling of a moist serpent and was beginning to like Pushkin.

My father's recitation was interrupted by applause. The gentleman was clapping loudly, but we soon saw that it was merely to alert his double, who now entered the compartment. 'Let him fetch tea and let it be boiling!' he instructed the man in the third person singular, as used between master and servant. The servant bowed and departed. Had he been chosen for a striking resemblance to his master, or had that happened naturally in the course of time? The gentleman now turned to my father. 'I admire any person of talent, even when he is an enemy and your poet was both. My grandfather was acquainted with him in St Petersburg. Alexandr Sergeyevich Pushkin was no friend of Poland! For a spirited poet, why not take our own national bard, Mickiewicz?' He began to recite a hunting scene in which the words brayed like dogs, horses galloped and horns echoed in the forest. I realised that the gentleman's speech too was declamatory, with phrases I had not heard before. My knowledge of Polish came from what I had learned at High School. I wondered whether I now heard it spoken in a style of an earlier, more elegant time.

The double returned with a jug of tea to which the gentleman added spirits in equal quantity from a silver flask, took gulps and offered some to my father. Cards were exchanged and my father henceforth addressed him as 'Count'. Conversation turned to political matters and to

112

a provincial governor, currently on trial for fraud, whom both the count and my father knew. I fell asleep. By the time I woke, the count and his double had left. A lady with a pretty girl in school uniform sat in his place. Her neat plaits were tied with white ribbons. But it was too late for conversation as the train had arrived in Lomza.

Parting from Fimek, who remained in town, my father and I walked to a long row of horse-carriages. The drivers, whips in their hands, crowded around us to undercut each other's prices. Despite the warm weather all were wrapped in long, black coats and wore heavy boots as though we had suddenly arrived into a winter we did not yet feel.

The dirt road to Lomzica, flanked with birch trees, must have been unchanged since my father's youth. The wheels creaked through mud, barking dogs chased us in the failing light as we trotted past broad fields and occasional wooden houses. We came to Lomzica in the dark. Dimly, I saw a cluster of houses, wooden fences and a pond through which the coachman had driven to the irate shrieking of geese. The relatives appeared ancient and bent, a tiny woman in black and a bearded man in a kaftan and skull-cap. They were brother and sister and owned the village grocery.

In the small, wooden house, a room with two beds, stacked high with quilts, was ready for us. I fell asleep by the light of a kerosene lamp and to an unbroken torrent of Yiddish, as the relatives brought my father up to date on village affairs. In the middle of the night I woke, my body itching and burning. By the kerosene light, I could see that I was covered in red spots and welts. I cried in pain and woke my father. The bed-sheet was stained with blood. When I turned the pillow, I saw small, fat insects marching in single file. 'Bedbugs,' said my father. He soaked a handkerchief in kerosene and wiped it over the welts. The itch abated slowly, but not my hysteria. We dragged the mattress onto the floor and surrounded it with a moat of kerosene until none remained in the lamp. Exhausted, I fell asleep again.

'Bedbugs are a fact of life here,' my father said the following morning, 'and it is bad taste to mention it. Eventually you get used to them, they get used to you and one arrives at a mutual understanding.' 'I'll burn my clothes,' I screamed with indignation, 'and I'll tell my mother!' Whereupon my father and I also arrived at a mutual understanding. He would drive with me to Lomza at noon, stock up on kerosene and take me to the cinema, while I would mention nothing to my mother. He kept his word and so did I.

Our return to Lomza was combined with a visit to my father's old professor. We went in search of him in a town about which I only recall open drains and a plague of frogs. Jumping, or squashed flat in large numbers, their stench pervaded the streets we walked through. In time, the professor was located, a frail man, semi-transparent like alabaster, with brown liver-spots on his bald head and hands. My father presented him with a Russian-French dictionary, bound in leather. The old man held it in his arms and wept.

A White Russian, who had remained in Poland, he addressed my father as 'Michael Zacharevich'. While they drank tea and conversed in Russian, I examined the bookshelves, his military epaulettes framed in glass, his icons and a large portrait of the Tsar and his daughters. From my experience of Fritz's library, I knew that the most interesting books were usually hidden in the rear. Here too, I was rewarded. The professor owned a cache of stiff, brown photographs in which fat, naked ladies posed as Greek goddesses, or held vases on their heads. From the other end of the room, I must have appeared to be a studious boy, and Michael Zacharevich was duly complimented on his son. 'I see you found the photographs,' said my father on our way to the cinema. 'When I was your age, I used to find them too.' We returned to Lomzica in the dark, carrying a large can of kerosene.

The relatives plied me with sweet carrots and boiled lentils and pinched my cheeks. Beyond that, we could not communicate. I was fascinated by the old lady's wig, which sat off-centre at a rakish angle, giving me hope that it might slide off. Her brother's beard covered much of his face, his mouth was invisible and his speech muffled, but judging by my father's amusement, their conversation was caustic and witty. They clearly loved 'little Mishka' and he had a real affection for them. All day, villagers came to sit with my father around the samovar, wanting to know about the 'big world' and about the Germans of whom there was now much talk. In the First World War, they had passed through Lomzica and were remembered kindly. One man came to do handstands on the table, wanting my father's advice on a career as an acrobat in America.

I rummaged through the grocery shop, located at the front of the house. A row of sacks were stacked along the walls. In the centre, stood a rough, wooden counter with a weighing machine. There was a variety of cereals, pepper, sugar and salt. 'Beggars are given lumps of sugar here instead of money,' my father had told me, 'and when their pockets are full, Uncle buys them back for a few kopeks.' Thus forewarned, I gave the sugar a miss. 'In earlier times, a large lump of sugar used to hang above this table and one licked it while drinking tea.' I assumed that my father was joking until I noticed a piece of string hanging over the dining table from a kerosene lamp above. Next to it, a mass of flies were struggling to free themselves from a ribbon of sticky paper. Those that succeeded fell into our meals.

There was nothing for me to do in our room. Apart from the beds and the wash-stand, the only furniture was a dark wardrobe, on which the door was little more than a large, jagged hole. My father explained that it had been hit by shrapnel in the First World War. Repair did not seem urgent. I walked about the dirt-roads chasing geese, ran between the tall sunflowers and was eyed with astonishment by the villagers for my outlandish clothes; short trousers and a beret. Like their sagging wooden houses, the people looked bent. Perhaps the young ones had left, or else some were still young under their beards and kaftans. Kerchiefs covered the women's heads, their dresses were grey, their shoes trodden down at the heels.

As it was a Friday, we accompanied the relative to the synagogue. It had been erected while my father had lodged in the village and I was told that my grandfather had therefore contributed generously to its construction. I expected a fine building. But like everything else it was neglected and ramshackle, and the bench I sat on collapsed under me. In their shining, Sabbath-best kaftans, the congregants swayed and bobbed as they prayed in the dim light and peered at me, as though my father had arrived with a dancing bear.

On the following Sabbath morning, the last of our stay, I accompanied my relative on a walk. As we passed a pond, a flaxen-haired boy, barefoot, in torn and ragged trousers, ran out from behind a fence, threw a stone and shouted, 'Filthy Jew!' at the old man. He walked on without turning his head. I took the stone, threw it back at the boy and pummelled him in Danzig street-style, one blow on each arm and a few more at his chest. I expected a good fight,

116

but he just stood there, like a sack in a boxing gym, waiting to be punched. I caught up with the old man who had marched ahead, rapidly and in silence. Back at the house, there was great commotion; Jewish boys did not hit people! Throwing a stone was work and I had broken the Sabbath! Beating up a Polish child, specially at Easter time, could lead to a pogrom and there had been enough of those in the past! I was sullen and angry. By leaving me in the lurch, then snitching to my father, the old man had also broken a few rules in my book.

The next day we returned to Lomza and the railway station. The coachman gave me the reins, while he chatted with my father in the rear. 'If there is war,' I heard him say, 'let the Russians come. It will be better for the Jews.' The train departed for Warsaw. Whatever warmth, wisdom and joy there had been in this *shtetl*, I had clearly missed it.

It rained on the return journey. The heavy drops obscured the windows of the carriage. The compartment was empty. In a few days I would be back at the school I did not like, among the Nazi uniforms in the streets and the tense faces of my relatives in Danzig. My father was pensive and moody. Passing through a seemingly endless forest, I asked him to tell me a story. It was the last one he ever told me and also the saddest:

A man comes to the Gate of Mercy and attempts to enter. A huge doorman, fierce like a Cossack, bars his way. 'Entry is forbidden!' May he wait? The doorman points to a kerbstone and the man sits down. He waits for weeks and years. In a moment of desperation, he decides to push the doorman aside and run through. The doorman seems to know the man's thoughts and laughs: 'Beyond this gate are other gates and before each, other doormen, taller and stronger than I. Get

117

back to the kerbstone!' More years pass and the man feels that he is fading away. As he slides prostrate to the ground, a terrible thought comes to him and he motions to the doorman. 'All men seek the Gate of Mercy,' he says with his last strength. 'Why in all these years has no one ever come here?' The doorman shouts into his ear, 'No one else could enter through this gate, because it was meant for you! Now I must go and close it.

I like to think that when my father died, he recognised the doorman from his youth in Lomzica and that he walked through the gate and took my mother with him.

The Lord Almighty

IN THE SPRING of 1939, the Central Synagogue which I passed on the way to school was being encased with a wooden hoarding. By the following day a banner had been hung above the Neo-Classic portico, proclaiming: 'This synagogue will be demolished.' On the hoarding, a larger sign read: '*Komm lieber Mai und mache von Juden uns jetzt frei!*' (Come dear May and liberate us from the Jews!) It seemed as though Danzig was preparing itself for a celebration.

The events which took me out of Danzig and saved my life were connected to that boarded-up synagogue, a relative who had died thirty years before and the Lord Almighty. That was the title by which Zvi Hermann Segal, a Polish merchant, was known to the Jews of Danzig. I had a worm's eye view of him when I accompanied a boy who delivered a letter to his house. His two daughters admitted us. We stood waiting in the hallway, while the younger one, who had recently discovered that boys were different from girls, kept prodding her fingers into our crotches with scientific curiosity. Time passed all too slowly. We were rescued by the arrival of the father, a gentleman in a dark suit, a gold watch-chain across his portly stomach and a Homburg hat pushed to the back of his head. I had seen the Lord Almighty.

There were suspicious whispers about Hermann Segal's

good relations with the Nazis. If wealthy Jews were jailed, he acted as middleman between the Gestapo and the arrested man's Swiss bank account. Miraculously, while little was known and less said, the arrested man would be released, to disappear from Danzig to wherever his visa admitted him. These and other deliverances gave Hermann Segal his divine reputation. He had come from Poland as an active 'Revisionist', the most militant in its demands for Palestine of all the Zionist groups.

The Revisionist Movement took its strength from the three million Jews of Poland and the urgency of their plight. Unlike the Socialist Zionism of the earlier Russian pioneers, Revisionists reflected the petty bourgeois society of Polish Jewry and had no sympathy with the concept of collective labour and the ideology of the kibbutz movement. Its founder, Zeev (Vladimir) Jabotinsky, envisioned a Jewish State on both sides of the Jordan River and its attainment by armed struggle against British and Arab opposition. The movement was influenced by the militant nationalism of postwar Poland, exemplified by Marshal Pilsudski. Jabotinsky himself was an admirer of Garibaldi and the Italian idealist D'Annunzio, who in turn influenced Mussolini.

A curious symbiosis existed between the anti-Semitic governments of Central Europe and the Revisionists. The former wanted to rid themselves of Jews, the latter wanted the Jews to be in Palestine. Both sides attempted to persuade the League of Nations to increase Jewish emigration to Palestine. Britain opposed it. It was the Revisionist perception that the enemy is not the one who wants you out of his home, but someone who bars you from entering yours. They therefore saw Britain as their major opponent and acted accordingly.

There was a similar understanding between Hermann

Segal and the Nazis of Danzig. Up to a point, their interests also overlapped. Years before, Jabotinsky had advocated the mass migration of Poland's Jews to Palestine; the idea had been treated with derision, a Messianic fantasy. What his disciple Segal now proposed was feasible. It is also possible that Segal's view of Poland's meagre chances in a war was realistic enough to assume that in time negotiations would have to take place between Germany and the Jews of Poland. The Holocaust, at that point, was still beyond anyone's grasp. What he negotiated with the Nazi government was the sale of the Jewish community's properties.

The money would be used for the migration of Danzig's remaining Jews. They would have to depart within six months, using the funds for transportation to Palestine, preferably with the authorisation of the British authorities. Should no entry permits be granted, they would attempt to do so illegally, evading the British blockade as best they could. Segal took this agreement to the Jewish community leaders early in 1938. Their suspicions of him and his Nazi connections caused them to reject it. They also anticipated little likelihood of British consent, while the attempt to enter Palestine illegally seemed to them both dangerous and irresponsible.

In November 1938, the two-day orgy of destruction by Stormtroopers on *Kristalnacht*, (the night of broken glass) brought with it mass arrests of Jews and great vandalism of their property, including the razing of two synagogues in the suburbs. The last of the Polish Jews in Danzig, numbering about fifteen hundred, fled across the border. The remaining two thousand Jews, all Danzig citizens, had no such option. In desperation, the community leaders reconsidered Segal and his plan. What had been foolhardy before seemed realistic now.

In December 1938, the Jewish community congregated in the Central Synagogue to be addressed by Hermann Segal. His message was terse and reflected the Revisionists' view: 'We are neither wanted here, nor strong enough to resist. Therefore we must leave. It is in our interest and also in the interest of the government of Danzig, to bring this about. When I last made this proposal to you, it was half an hour to midnight. Now it is one minute to midnight and your last chance. Do not miss it!' The congregation of two thousand rose in silence to signal their consent. The Nazis now offered a pittance for the properties of the community. With no alternative, it had to be accepted.

But there was to be an additional financial source to help the 'Segal Plan'. In 1910, shortly before his death, Lesser Gielinski, a patrician grain-merchant and a relative of our family, willed his collection of Jewish ceremonial art and precious porcelain to the community. The collection was housed in the synagogue. Its purpose, he wrote, 'was to give pleasure to me and others.' The collection was famous among connoisseurs, including the German Royal Family, which had also decorated Gielinski for his lifelong philanthropy. Additional money was raised by auctioning the porcelain collection in Berlin, while an American source agreed to acquire the Judaica and house it in the Jewish Theological Seminary in New York.

Hoping to obtain British consent for entry to Palestine, the head of Danzig's Jewish community, Dr Itzig, travelled to London. He argued that as Danzig was a ward of the League of Nations, which had also granted Britain the original Mandate to administer Palestine, the Jews of Danzig should be given special consideration. He found no help from any source. On his return, he related details of a meeting with Lord Rothschild, whose aid he had sought, 'in the matter of the Jewish Question.' 'I know only an English Question,' had been the reply, 'and Jewish immigration to Palestine is not in its interest.'

Illegal immigration was now the only course of action and the Nazis were willing to connive in it. Although it was of no consequence to them whether ships full of Jews sailed or sunk, if they did reach their destination there would be some political gain for Germany. The British government was attempting to win Arab support in the anticipated war by blocking Jewish immigration. The arrival of more refugees would cause them embarrassment by further antagonising the Arabs.

During his London visit, Dr Itzig also contacted volunteer organisations active in bringing Jewish children from Germany and Austria to England. He managed to include the children of Danzig in this project. A total of ten thousand children below the age of sixteen were granted entry in to England. They were admitted as 'travelling to an unspecified destination, provided that they would not be a financial burden on the government.' The volunteer organisations had been arranging transport for groups of children from various towns and placing them in foster homes. As the children of Danzig were too young for the hazards of an illegal voyage to Palestine, this permit came at an opportune time. Financed with the money raised by the 'Segal Plan', two groups of children departed early in 1939. A final group left on 25 August, days before the outbreak of war. I was in that last group.

Meanwhile Hermann Segal, with Nazi connivance, had made arrangements for the overland departure of seven hundred immigrants to Romania, where they embarked on a small, over-crowded vessel, the *Astir*. On reaching Haifa, the vessel was turned back by the British Navy. It then meandered aimlessly for over two months in vile and unsanitary conditions, under British air-surveillance.

Finally a second landing was attempted, scuttling the ship off the Gaza Coast. The captain was able to invoke the Law of the Sea, applying to sinking ships. The journey had taken three months, but it had achieved its aim.

A second group of people organised by Hermann Segal, left Romania in a paddle-steamer in 1941. It was not as fortunate. After its arrival off the coast of Haifa, British troops transferred the refugees to another vessel for transport to an interment camp in Mauritius. The Jewish Underground decided to disable the ship, to prevent its departure. The explosives they planted sunk the vessel, drowning two hundred people. The survivors were shipped off to Mauritius where they spent five years, before returning to a Palestine, which by then was about to become Israel.

Despite hardships and tragedy en route, the majority of Danzig's Jews were saved from the coming Holocaust. In no small part, this was due to Hermann Segal. He was a man whose actions saved the lives of many people. A man who manipulated and negotiated as an intermediary between the Nazis and wealthy Jews. He was someone the Nazis trusted, the Jew with whom they could do business for their cause as well as for themselves. Segal also did business for himself, as well as for his cause, that of populating Palestine with Jews. In Steven Spielberg's film *Schindler's List*, many of those whom Schindler saved are shown awaiting him on his arrival in Israel to express their gratitude. Many people owe a similar debt to Hermann Segal, and I am one of them.

Hermann Zvi Segal, too, reached Palestine and continued his political involvement as a Revisionist. He became a member of *Etzel*, the underground organisation that was eventually headed by Menachem Begin. Arrested by the British authorities, he was deported to Kenya during the war. As a member of parliament upon the establishment of the State of Israel he was signatory to the Declaration of Independence.

Thereafter Segal purchased a large tract of land in what today is the town of Ashkelon. His dream was to build a film city there; a second Hollywood. It never materialised and before his death in 1965 he had lost most of his money. On the sandy coastal land he owned, Segal built a lone café and called it 'Casino'. Was it in memory of Danzig's great casino on the Baltic shore, or of the greater game of chance he played with the Nazis?

The Danzig collection of Judaica still travels around the world, as though in search of its original resting-place. Billed as 'The Treasures of a Lost Community', I have encountered it over the years in museums in New York, Chicago, Tel Aviv and Los Angeles. A bitter meaning has been given to Lesser Gielinski's wish that 'it should give pleasure to me and others.' In the Jewish religious objects I design, I try to pay my respects to this last vestige of the community I belonged to.

On the day that the last sixteen children left Danzig for London, air-raid sirens were being tested on the rooftops of the city. The main streets were full of tourists with military haircuts and identical suits, taking great interest in the layout of the city. A group of them asked my mother for directions as we waited for a taxi to take us to the meeting point from which the childrens' transport departed Danzig.

A label around my neck, I arrived in London and stood on Waterloo Station two days later. It was a cold, foggy morning and the small group of children with whom I had made the journey were soon dispersed among the waiting grown-ups, who carried gas masks. Here too, the air-raid sirens were being tested. Their high-pitched scream sounded in relays throughout the city. Though we had no knowledge of the language and the people, it was clear to us that war was expected and the tension was obvious. My mother's two sisters, Elschen and Ruth, were among the grown-ups waiting to take me home. I think I also became a grown-up from that day on.

I have been very fortunate in my life, having a wife, two fine children and more good friends than I deserve. I love my work and live comfortably. I have seen many aspects of life, some beautiful, some abhorrent, in different parts of the world. I have also survived six wars, in three of which I was a soldier. It diminishes none of this if I say that the sun was never as bright, the light as penetrating or the visions so memorable, the sadness so terrible, as in those days, in those streets and houses, with those people, who have all vanished forever.

When the Tourists Came

WITHIN FORTY-EIGHT hours of my departure, acting by night, the Nazi authorities arrested all Polish residents in Danzig. The operation was co-ordinated with the German Army, which a day later crossed the Polish border. The tourists with military haircuts whom I had seen on the streets before I left, had been German soldiers familiarising themselves with the layout of the city they were about to annex. Danzig was incorporated into the Reich to the jubilant cheers of its population. The Gestapo had prepared the night arrests of the Poles long in advance. A list of everyone had been compiled from details supplied by German neighbours.

A special unit concerned itself with the students and teachers of the Polish High School, as well as with intellectuals, artists and members of Polish associations, down to the Boy Scouts. A detailed dossier on all these had been compiled by the man who now came out of the shadows – Mr Wendrowski, our art teacher. A member of the SS, he had been infiltrated into the school for this purpose. No doubt my name was also on this list. 'The secret lies in the shadows,' Mr Wendrowski taught us. If one had pencilled in the shadows around him, would the profile of an SS man have emerged? At the end of the war, the Polish authorities caught Mr Wendrowski and he was sent to the gallows. He was responsible for many deaths. But death

127

throws no shadows.

A number of teachers and older students were immediately shot. The Polish post office, which had so offended the Nazis with its recent issue of stamps, was attacked in a sham military action and the personnel were executed. Most of those arrested were taken to the nearby village of Stutthof, selected by the SS as a suitable site for a concentration camp to serve Danzig, Kashubia and Pomerania. The prisoners were forced to build the camp, starting with rows of wooden huts; many were starved and worked to death. Stutthof was one of Germany's least-known concentration camps. Situated to the northeast of Danzig, it was hemmed in by the dunes of the Baltic and the Vistula river, while a convenient railway track ended there. It was policed by the SS, who in time embellished it with the usual machinery of extermination: torture rooms, gas chambers and a crematorium.

Over a hundred thousand people perished in Stutthof, including the teachers and students of Petershagen, the last few hundred Jews of Danzig, Polish soldiers, dissidents from the surrounding countryside and others. The inmates were sent as slave labour to Danzig, in their striped pyjamas, to die of malnutrition in full view of the town's inhabitants. They laboured in quarries, brickyards, dyke repairs, in the poison-gas plant and in the shipyards, later to become famous as the Lenin Shipbuilding Yards. Many respectable firms used them as slave labour. Some remain German enterprises of good repute to this day.

In the centre of Danzig, at the Academy of Medicine, a Professor Spanner received regular supplies of fresh bodies executed in Stutthof. Dissected and boiled in vats with caustic soda, the inventive professor manufactured soap from them based on a special recipe and kept the Danzig authorities informed on his progress. In the end, the

remains of hundreds of corpses were found in his laboratory by the invading Russian army. The professor had left
earlier for Germany on a lecture tour, where he presum-
ably embarked on a postwar career in another line of
research.

Meanwhile, a German organisation named 'Head Office
for Race and Settlement' concerned itself with Kashubian
and Polish children under the age of thirteen. Its priority
was to carry out Hitler's dictum: 'To Germanise the land
and exterminate what was not usable.' Children with blue
eyes, blond hair and the right skull dimensions would be
classified as 'racially useful material'. Those selected were
taken to brutal training camps where they were taught the
benefits of being second-class Germans. Suitable girls in
that category were taken to breeding-farms, injected with
hormones to speed puberty, impregnated by SS men and
put to death after the second or third child. As for the rest,
Hitler in theory and Himmler in practice had only one use
for Poles – to turn them into menial labourers. The next
generation would be taught only to write their names,
count to five hundred, and show proper respect to
Germans.

Little today remains of the Polish High School at
Petershagen. In postwar Gdansk, the building still stands.
It has another function now, and time has turned it grey
and sad. The street it stands on has lost its German name
and is now Augustinski Street in memory of the murdered
headmaster. One room has been set aside as a memorial,
with faded photographs of pupils flanked by their teachers. I looked at faces I had last seen fifty years ago. There
was Pawel in his scout's uniform with his pasty face, ready
to call me a 'dirty *zyd*'. There was Bolek who copied my
Latin homework, and Professor Urbanek who escaped the
Germans and distinguished himself in the war. I saw the

shy, petite girl whom I adored and never spoke to, until the day after *Kristalnacht* when we walked together to her father's gutted shop in the Kashubian market, and saw her parents sitting helpless amid the rubble.

I realised with the passing years, that at the Polish school I had learned something about the history and culture which had bound my fellow pupils and teachers together. Generations of resistance to occupation and the urge to retain their identity, had created a code that Poles were able to share. Legends of the insurrections and their heroism were its milestones. I knew that this was not a domain I could enter, nor did I want to. But when in the 1980s, I watched the televised debates between the Communist leaders of Poland and the striking workers at the Gdansk shipyards, I understood the coded words they used. 'Let us talk Pole to Pole' (*Polak do Polaka*), a phrase which meant 'let us whisper to each other and find ways to avoid another invasion by a Russian army.' I had learned these nuances, although I remained an interloper.

I came to that school a stranger and was certainly a misfit, though who would have noticed one more in a city that was itself a misfit? But I would have wished a better life and, in the fullness of time, a better death for the students and teachers than that inflicted on them by the Germans and those good people, the citizens of Danzig.

'To Be an Englishman'

THE BUS DREW OUT, taking us away from Danzig. Did anyone realise the finality of that moment? Among the sixteen children, some cried, all were sad. We crossed into Germany, boarding a train for Berlin and the Dutch border, a day's journey ahead. In Berlin, in the early morning, a cousin whom my mother must have alerted, stood waiting on the platform with fruit for everyone. Some hours later, the Gestapo official passed through our compartments, noted down names and confided that we would find London drab and foggy, 'not like beautiful Paris'. He shook hands, said *'Gute Reise'* (pleasant journey), and descended at the German side of the border.

Passing through Dutch countryside in the afternoon sun, we were more excited and cheerful. Someone said that Dutch tidiness included curtains on the windows of cowsheds. We tried to catch a glimpse of them from the speeding train. At the next station, I heard my first word of Dutch, *'Verscheklich!'* (Terrible!). It was said by a mother, when pointing us out to her child. Hearing this from a stranger, I had the uneasy sense, for the first time, that more might be involved in our departure than a temporary separation. A night-ferry carried us from the Hook of Holland to Harwich. It tossed about in the Channel. Nausea prevented us from sleeping. The sailors, who had no such problems, attempted to flirt with the two or three

131

older girls in our group. One of them was sick over a sailor's uniform and the rest withdrew in haste. In the morning, a train delivered us to London, tired and in great need of a bath.

There had been a transient feeling, despite our sadness, that we were on a holiday excursion. But excursions come to an end and this one never did. In some way, all of us are still travelling.

With a grandmother and two aunts awaiting me, I was more fortunate than most of the other children. My mother's older sister, Ruth, was married to Kurt Regan, the doctor from Bavaria who had recently established his practice in Harley Street. Kurt spoke with the same, soft Bavarian accent as his younger brother Fritz, but was more assertive, emphasised by the duelling scars on his cheek, a souvenir from student days. He had seen enough of the Nazis in Bavaria to be persuaded to move his family to England.

He had emigrated with his wife, son, mother, mother-in-law and sister-in-law. They lived in adjacent apartments in Putney, not far from the Thames. It could not have been easy to be responsible for them all, and my arrival added to the burden. My father had been able to transfer money for me, but as the war far outlasted the few months of hostilities he had predicted, I soon became another of Kurt's expenses. It says much for him that I was never made to feel it.

Kurt's loyalties were uneasily divided between pre-Nazi Germany and his new country. Thoroughly German, he had been an officer on the Russian front in the First World War and been decorated for bravery by the white-haired King of Bavaria. Any mention of Germany's responsibility for that would infuriate him. '*Ach, Quatsch!*' (rubbish!), he shouted, when I brought up the bayoneting of Belgian

132

babies by German soldiers. 'Nothing but vile lies!' At the time I ascribed his reaction to blind patriotism. But as I write these words, it was revealed that Kurt had been right. The British War Office only recently announced, eighty years after the event, that it had indeed created the legend to inflame British public opinion against Germany.

In his Harley Street surgery, the British War Office, inventive as ever, had forced Kurt to line the inner walls with wire-mesh to prevent him from using his X-ray machine to send messages to the Nazis. It would have had a similar preventative effect had they fenced in his lavatory seat.

In time, Kurt acquired an impressive array of diplomats and film stars as patients. He was a handsome, dapper man, always elegant, and women found him attractive. Kurt reciprocated the compliment. Among his female admirers, I remember the actress Lilli Palmer as well as Rex Harrison, her husband at the time. There was also a very infatuated Austrian princess, whose illustrious ancestor, Prince Windisch-Grätz, had done much butchery with his troops in Italy.

Kurt and Ruth's only child, Nils, was my first cousin, a year older than I and on his way to being very English. He was already at school and arrangements had to be made now for my education. I had learned a little English from Professor Urbanek in Danzig. At an interview, the headmaster of the school I was to attend said to my uncle, 'I am interested in the boy. I'll take him if he can learn sufficient English by next term.'

In the following weeks, I went to the home of Professor Bonelli for a language class with a small group of other boys. The professor, who was short and stout, usually dressed in black clothes of a military cut, had a strong Italian accent. We were told that we were not meant to speak as he did, but to practise what he would teach us. The teaching method was phonetic. The mouth was a wind instrument and by moving the tongue to different positions, according to Professor Bonelli's instructions, perfect English would eventually emerge. The grammar he taught and the vocabulary we had to learn at home, were the musical notes our mouths would play to cultivate elegant diction and inspire respect.

The sounds we had to practice on our newly discovered instrument were carefully modulated passages from *The Betrothed*, an English translation of Alessandro Manzoni's classic *I Promessi Sposi*. We recited the lines spoken by Lucia who loved Renzo and was thwarted by the villain Don Rodrigo. When the translation seemed inadequate, the Professor, apparently forgetting that we were meant to learn English, lapsed into the original; '*Addio, monti surgenti dall' acque . . . addio casa natia*', and in the voice of the plotting villain: '*Questo matrimonio non s'ha da fare, ne domani, ne mai!*' (this marriage shall not take place, neither tomorrow nor ever!).

On the walls were portraits of King Victor-Emmanuel, Giuseppe Mazzini, and the stern profile of Benito Mussolini. A white bust of Cavour stood in a corner. The professor explained them all to us, from the history of the Risorgimento which united Italy, to Mussolini, who had restored the country to its rightful place in the world. 'All men of courage! Please raise the tongue to the roof of your mouth and slowly breathe out the word: C-O-U-R-A-G-E.'

Among the professor's pupils was Heinz, a boy recently arrived from Berlin with whom I formed a lasting friendship. He had just turned sixteen, an age at which one was classified as an Enemy Alien and had to register with the local police. 'What was your previous address?' asked the constable behind the desk. 'Please sir, Kant Street, Berlin.'

'Why you filthy little bugger!' shouted the officer and threw him out. Heinz, who had no idea what he had done, was very agitated. As my cousin had already initiated me into the new vocabulary, I was able to explain.

The weeks passed. One day I arrived at Professor Bonelli's home for my usual lesson and found that I no longer had a teacher. He had been arrested at night as an 'Enemy Alien' and taken to an unknown destination. As a dedicated fascist he had, it seemed, received special attention because his belongings were strewn about on the floor and the pupils helped an agitated Italian to pack them into cases. The pictures of his heroes had disappeared from the wall.

My phonetic lessons had come to an end, but I was judged sufficiently advanced by the headmaster to attend school. No matter how much I moved the tongue about in my mouth, breathed and blew, I never did acquire the English accent that inspired respect. Nor did I ever find out whether Renzo married Lucia. Perhaps in some internment camp a group of assorted enemy agents and spies graduated under the professor's guidance to become English gentlemen. In any case – *Addio, Professore Bonelli e mille grazie*!

I was to spend three-and-a-half years at a private high school in the northern outskirts of London. I lived on the premises, with a number of other boarders. Since then, the days of the week have always been marked for me by puddings. Bread and Butter Pudding was eaten on Mondays, on Wednesdays it was Rice Pudding and Treacle Tart made the Sabbath holy. The school was close to an older, more famous one called Harrow where Winston Churchill had been a below-average pupil. Cutting through the suburban high street and surrounding houses, one came to a landscape of green meadows and a small forest, Harrow on the Hill. A cemetery lay there, with a bench facing the skyline of distant London. I often took my homework to that bench and a year later, when air-raids became nightly events, I sat there and watched London burn.

Our school principal was a retired bishop, who had spent most of his life in West Africa. The climate had turned his face the colour of tanned leather. His high fore-head, lined face and the uptilt of his nose, resembled a Gothic sculpture. He had bright, warm eyes and a cynical wit: 'Geography assumes a very special meaning when one serves the Lord in the anus of the world.' He was fond of whisky and it must have been his only pleasure during those decades in Africa. At sunset, he raised the first of many glasses, with the inevitable toast, 'God smite Hitler and all his dirty deeds!' I think he regarded this as his con-tribution to the war effort.

The bishop had faith in the Apostolic Succession, of which he was a part. A long line of bishops had anointed each other through two millennia, reaching back to St Peter himself. He felt that through this pipeline, he had access to the ear of God. Both he and his wife, who was responsible for the welfare of the boarders, were kind people. Their religion was the practice of decency, in con-trast to the Church-inspired bigotry that had made life at my Polish school so difficult. 'You carry your religion, I carry mine, both are judged on where we take them,' he told me once and the subject was never discussed again. However, I did enjoy the morning hymns about 'Jerusalem the Golden' and the 'Green Hill Far Away', which he led in a strong baritone, while his wife played on an harmonium before a ragged choir of pupils. Urged on by the bishop, his wife and the harmonium, many generations of Hausas

136

and Yorubas must have raised their voices skyward to 'Hymns Ancient and Modern'.

We were to learn much from him about the Gold Coast, its climate, tribes, ritual scars, female circumcision and the symbolism of tribal carvings. The bishop had a collection of ebony sculptures which were part of the school museum. Eventually, I became its curator and learned to admire African carvings. I liked the Benin Bronzes, where a large chief, on a small horse – or was it a large dog? – held two tiny servants by the throat. It was a finely-crafted example of status dictating size.

I entered the school early in 1940. Most teachers had been conscripted into the army. They were replaced by teachers resuming their profession after years in retirement. If they were a little old-fashioned, idiosyncratic and forgetful, it was like a holiday to me after the schools of Danzig. The tensions I had learned to expect were absent. One did not have to bark 'Herr Professor!' to the teacher while standing to attention. His proper name sufficed, he seemed human and one could reply to him while seated. The pupils, too, were friendly to a newcomer trying to learn the language, which made adjustment easier. I soon realised that geography and especially history had a different emphasis. They dealt with the British Isles, of which I knew nothing, and those large pink coloured parts on the globe, the British Empire. There was greater stress on social and economic issues rather than battles, rulers and patriotic slogans. I struggled with the language and more complex still, tried to understand *As You Like It*, in which I had a minor part in the coming school play. The bishop obviously believed in throwing me in at the deep end.

As page to the exiled Duke, my lines were few. 'Say it like a German,' I was instructed by the teacher directing the play. 'Bow from the hips and click your heels. You are a German boy, sent to a foreign court to learn their ways.' Released from the shackles of Shakespearean diction, I did as directed. Turning to Touchstone, I bawled out my lines: 'You are deceived, Sir! Ve kept time! Ve lost not our time!' Touchstone shrunk back in fright.

The spirit of the times was upon us. From Elstree Studios to Hollywood, film agents were leafing through directories in search of screen Germans. Men with sausage lips, blue eyes and peroxide in their hair, began to make a good living. They wore tight uniforms, clicked their heels, looked up at maps on the wall, sneered at prisoners and fell to the floor with multiple jerks when Allied bullets hit them at the end of the film. Over the years one became familiar with their faces. They belonged to a select club of fear-inspiring men. In time they were joined by Filipinos with false buck-teeth, the screen Japanese, whose expertise lay in falling out of palm trees.

Many years later, sitting on the terrace of my home in Jaffa, the bell rang and the SS man of many a tense war drama stood before me. The sausage lips, pale blue eyes and arrogant nose were all in place. His hand was stretched out. I assumed that he would demand to see my papers, but we shook hands instead. Herr Hardy Kruger, the quintessential film Nazi, had come to work in Israel. We had mutual friends. We sipped drinks, looked over the terrace onto the Mediterranean and spoke about our friends. Mr Kruger was a courteous man, but for the rest of his visit I had trouble with my vision of him, like a photographer who cannot quite focus the lens of his camera on an illusive object.

At school, I walked about with a pocket dictionary which I pulled out at critical moments. It was not easy to win an argument 'game, set and match' if one had to look up even those three words. Amusement over my problems was generally good-natured. 'Never mind old chap, you'll get it right in the end.' I learned that rather than gleefully jumping up and down when winning a game, one was expected to look funereal and say 'hard luck, old man' to the loser. It was correct to dismiss one's victory at table tennis, 'it was only a fluke', and then run into the privacy of the toilet to jump for joy. Asked 'how did the exams go?' the answer was 'not so well, actually,' which was code for 'a damn sight better than yours, I hope!' I had to make up for lost time and learn to become diffident, so that my behaviour would appear as inconspicuous as the grey flannel uniforms which hid our egos. That, it seemed, was the English way, which foreigners confused with hypocrisy. 'One never knows out of which sleeve an Englishman's hand will emerge', said the wealthy Indian merchant with whose son I studied, when he saw us practising diffidence. 'When the same can be said about you, you'll have graduated.'

Like Afghan polo, which is played with the head of a sheep, love of cricket has to be acquired early. I came to it too late. Instead, I enjoyed the combination of strategy, team work and violence of football, and the hot Ovaltine that came after.

Time passed and the phoney war became real. France collapsed and the air-raids began. We experienced them as sirens in the night, searchlights prodding the clouds, the thud of guns shooting into the sky and the whistle of falling bombs. I received postcards from my parents. They were sent on by a relative in neutral Lithuania, and re-addressed to me. I replied in the same way. The words were uniformly bland, 'We are well – Write!' Only the handwriting and the green ink which my father habitually used were recognisable. The fear that accompanied those sentences was not. My mother had joined my father in

Warsaw, but the address was unfamiliar. I thought that it would please them to see me in school uniform and went up the hill to the studio of a photographer who specialised in portraits for the neighbouring schools. I still have the copy. The emblem on my blazer read '*Regnat Deus*' (God Reigns). It must have seemed a cruel joke to anyone who saw it in the Warsaw Ghetto. The relative in Lithuania was someone I had never heard of before. When war broke out between Germany and the Soviet Union, Lithuania became a battlefield. No more cards arrived. After the war I learned that he too had been killed.

There were periods when homesickness came like a black wave of depression. I sat down then, in a corner of the little school museum and drew Danzig, as I had done with Peter long before. I drew the Dutch gables, the stone stairs and the gargoyles that spouted water in the rain. I often dreamed of walking familiar streets, looking through familiar windows. Infrequently that dream still returns and brings with it a curious tranquillity. Long after the amputation of a leg, the non-existent toes still itch. Long after its destruction, one's home still pretends to be waiting. Perhaps my sculptures today, the clustered buildings I shape, the figures I create, are a continuation of this need. Images handed on through the memory of a child, to the technique of an adult.

My relatives in London could not come to visit me at school. Though they were not interned as Germans, their movements were restricted. The school lay outside their permitted area. On my visits to them, my grandmother and aunts played checkers and cards with me, a sure way to increase my pocket money. I also met family friends and heard the latest gossip of refugee life. Uneasy rumours were circulating about camps which the Germans were building in Poland.

Living in Putney, close to the Thames, German planes frequently flew over at night. The moonlight reflecting on the water was their guide for the homeward run. Often the last bombs were dropped indiscriminately over the adjacent suburbs and the buildings shook with the explosions. The green pebbled tennis-courts were studded with rusting shrapnel. When an air-raid became intense, my aunts would shake me awake. We assembled in the bathroom. Built of concrete and windowless, it was considered the safest part of the house. We were a bizarre ensemble. The ladies sat on the edge of the bath in furs and pearls, jewellery bulging in sequinned handbags. Kurt sat on the toilet, in an elegant suit, pearl tie-pin, his wallet full of cash. It was rumoured that rescue crews were not adverse to taking whatever they found in the rubble and what one carried on one's person was more secure. We sat in silence under the gloomy bathroom light, figures out of a Berlin Theatre of the Absurd or a macabre painting by Otto Dix, waiting for the ceiling to collapse. But it never did and I returned to school, an area of less interest to the Luftwaffe.

At Christmas time in 1942, our school went to the theatre. The play was *Puss in Boots*, a traditional pantomime. The Principal Boy was a girl, with such long and shapely legs that it was difficult to concentrate on the play. The safety curtain descended during the interval. My friends ran off to queue for ice cream. I remained in my seat, cold with anxiety, the blood in my head pounding. As the actress danced among the cardboard foliage and the Big Cat cavorted, I had suddenly understood that I was an orphan. I repeated the word many times, as one tries on an image, or a suit of uncertain shape. To me, orphans were Dickensian waifs, kept in grim institutions, taught to know their position and be humble. It was not an image I accepted for myself. For some time, I had experienced a growing anxiety that I might never see my parents again. Mail no longer came from them and on my visits to Putney I heard terrifying rumours about extermination camps. These rumours, which reached me even as a child at school, appeared to be of little interest to any government. The Polish Underground had given extensive details about the camps to their government-in-exile in London. They were ignored in Washington and London.

In protest at indifference to the unfolding Holocaust, a lone member of the Polish government-in-exile committed suicide. In his suicide note, he wrote: 'The responsibility for the crime of murdering the whole Jewish population of Poland rests in the first place with the murderers themselves, but indirectly, it rests upon all humanity, the government and peoples of the Allied States, which have not yet undertaken any concerted action to stop this crime.' These words were written at a time when 300,000 out of Poland's pre-war Jewish population of 3.3 million were still alive. Little more than a year later, ninety per cent of those had also been exterminated. The only recognition of his act was to name a street in his memory, three decades later, in Tel Aviv.

I realised that even if my parents survived these ordeals, they would be sick and broken people in need of my support. I had to prepare myself for either case. I felt envious of those around me who had the support and guidance of their family. All I could recall were my father's words at Warsaw Station: 'Study hard, go to university, don't be like Uncle Fimek.' I decided to follow that advice to the end.

At the next interval, I ran off to buy an ice cream. The crisis had passed. 'Bugger the waif, I'll be a fighting orphan!'

*

By 1943 I had passed the exams which, once the war was over, would allow me to enter university. The final school year was intense, with swotting and rehearsals with examination papers of previous years. The war and the bombing were also intense. Passing through Central London one day, I witnessed the results of the previous night's destruction in Oxford Street, with large buildings reduced to smoking ruins. Sawdust had been spread on the pavements to soak up blood. By evening, the city's underground stations were crowded with people sheltering from the nightly bombing. Families lay under eiderdowns and blankets. Entertainers walked among them, playing 'Knees up Mother Brown' on their accordions. One had to step carefully between hands and feet, to reach the train. Henry Moore depicts these scenes in his famous 'Shelter drawings' as solid bodies stacked side by side. It is a curiously cold exercise in abstract forms, which misses the tension and camaraderie of the people he drew.

Walking home towards my aunt's in Putney one late winter evening, air-raid sirens sounded, followed immediately by the piercing whistle of bombs directly overhead. I threw myself to the ground, at the side of a low brick wall. There was a loud explosion and a strong rush of air passed over the garden wall, rolling me across the pavement. In a surreal silence, flames rose above the low rooftops of houses one street beyond. I had missed a direct hit, but others had not. With unsteady legs, I got up, stumbled over bricks blown off the wall and, running along the road, came to an intersection, where I saw a solitary truck. Recovering from shock, the driver was resting his head on the steering wheel. His truck had been blown into the air and fallen back on its wheels. I sat next to him in the dark cabin, as ambulances and fire engines sped past. The fires in the adjacent road were spreading. The driver was a Scot and had driven down from Glasgow. I strained to understand his accent. He talked to me about his life, I told him about mine. Although we barely saw each other's faces, we spoke like old friends. Over an hour passed before he felt able to drive and he took me home.

The arm and leg I had scraped in the fall soon healed, but I often dreamed of a silent blast of wind lifting my body over rooftops. I always awoke with a start when it was time to crash.

The last year of final exams was tense with work, grim with air-raids and worry about my parents. And yet, as in a fairy tale, two doors suddenly materialised before me. One was labelled 'Perspective', the other 'Sex'. Unlike the fateful doors of fairy tales, I could enter both at once.

In the school library, I discovered a book on perspective. It illustrated how, with a nail and string, one could establish Vanishing Points on drawings and so create depth and distance in them. It was a great revelation which I practised with a sketch-book wherever possible. I drew the eye-view of a worm, looking at the shoe about to descend, of a bird looking down from a church steeple and the idealised vista of the high street, with the Odeon Cinema closing the prospect, like a Roman Hippodrome, flanked by temples and statues. The Renaissance painter Uccello, credited with this invention, was said to have driven his wife insane with his addictive discovery. I merely succeeded in boring my friends and relatives. But I was now on the path that, for better or worse, would lead to architecture.

The second door was opened by a boy in my class, when he proposed a double-date to the cinema. I was flattered but not surprised. With his shaven eyebrows and a coiled serpent tattooed on his belly, Steven was ahead of us all in self-confidence and initiative. He had discovered a billiard-hall, frequented by truck-drivers, where no one pointed to the door when we asked to rent a table. We played there in raincoats to hide our school uniforms, amid tough men, beer mugs and cigarette fumes. The camaraderie of the open road seemed to protect us from awkward questions, as long as we did not push our luck by asking for beer.

Steven had not merely acquired a girlfriend from the neighbourhood who liked going 'all the way', but also a friend of hers with a similar proclivity. I wondered whether to shave my eyebrows, and practice the slow, rolling shoulder movements of truck-drivers, and examined my pocket money. The accumulated gains at the card table in Putney would now be put to fitting use. The path from gambling to women seemed a natural progression. I had enough for two cinema tickets, fish and chips and a bottle of Tizer.

On a sunny Saturday afternoon, we walked into the back garden of a suburban home, where a group of Air Force officers sat around a beautiful dark-haired girl, in a bathing-suit. Her long legs splashed the water in a rubber swimming pool. She was the older sister of Steven's girl, daughters of a professional officer in the Air Force. Ignored by the group, we sat down to wait on nearby deck-chairs. I felt as uncertain of my role as someone admitted to Paradise through the tradesman's entrance. Steven's nonchalance could only have come from the serpent on his belly. We waited, listening to the laughter and clinking of glasses from the poolside. Then, suddenly, our girls were there in flowered dresses, amid a whiff of Lily of the Valley, which I remembered my mother wore. Steven kissed his dark, slim girl and I met Annie, her friend, blonde with almond eyes, a little plump and very pretty. Both girls wore adult make-up. Beige cream on their legs simulated silk stockings, unavailable in wartime England.

A black line went up the calf of each leg, in imitation of a seam. I wondered how far up it went. Before we left, Steven winked in my direction with thumbs up. Unnoticed by me, the girls had signalled that I would do.

In the cinema, with my arms around Annie and her hands doing wondrous things in my lap, we watched a Chicago gangster inherit a dukedom through distant family connections. The back rows in which we sat resounded to the sounds of urgent whispers, kisses and creaking seats. Above us, through a hole in the wall, a beam of light transformed itself into pictures on the screen. The back rows had experienced a frustrating hiatus, while a floodlit organ rose out of the orchestra pit and a man in a white suit made the auditorium reverberate with patriotic music. 'We're going to hang our washing on the Siegfried Line, have you any dirty washing, mother dear?' The lyrics were on the screen for all to sing. Then darkness fell again. The gangster came to loot the estate, but the loyalty of family-retainers, the love of the game-keeper's daughter and the assertion of his blue blood, converted him into an aristocrat. With Annie's help, I also came into my inheritance. We embraced and kissed before and after our fish and chips and in every accessible doorway from there to her home. There was a wonderfully stormy time the following weekend on the couch, in the house of Steven's girl. I discovered that Annie's almond eyes came from a Chinese grandfather. She claimed to see in the dark with them. Looking into them, I imagined Chinese ancestors peering with disapproval at the red-faced foreign devil who clung to their progeny. We had other exciting evenings at the cinema, a night in the cemetery at Harrow on the Hill and in an Air Force officer's parked car near the house. Sometimes we had ice cream in the next-door café and held hands under the table, waiting for the weekend to come.

Suddenly, there came a Saturday when both girls were busy. Simultaneously, a new species of uniformed men made their appearance on the streets, leaning against walls in groups and chewing gum. From their rakish caps to their brown boots, they had smarter clothes than the rough blanket-like khaki of British soldiers. Military trucks and jeeps with white stars drove about in the high street. An American base had opened in the vicinity. A corporal, leaning against a lamppost, handed me a Hershey Bar and said, 'Hi there, I'm Hank Waggoner.' Hank perhaps was among those who now regularly took Annie and Steven's girl to the Rainbow Club in Shaftesbury Avenue. They were always busy, and I saw that Annie wore real silk stockings.

A second disaster struck. We were expelled from the billiard hall, blamed for damage done to a green baize table cover. Only school work was left to us. I noticed that Steven's eyebrows were growing again.

It was at this time that the English accent I was acquiring stopped in its tracks. In conversation with guests in the home of Steven's girl, an Air Force officer interrupted to correct my pronunciation. It was an act of kindness which I politely obeyed, while inwardly in a rage. He seemed to point me along a path I did not want to take – to be like him. I felt that I would thereby cross a divide which, however narrow, would leave my past on the other side. I would become a different person, a fake to myself and those I had left behind.

What followed was not a conscious decision but it seems that I had made a pact with my accent and it would remain. 'I detect a foreign intonation', I am frequently told. 'Central European perhaps?' And that is as it should be. Years later, I heard that Annie became a GI bride and went to live in Alaska. While I was at university a postcard from her reached me by a circuitous route.

By the time the exam results were published, I was far away. Apparently I had obtained the highest marks in my school that year, but there was no longer anyone to whom I could say, 'It was just a fluke, old chap'; neither did I jump for joy. The rules had changed.

Interlude

'NOW THAT YOU are no longer a schoolboy, the authorities will regard you as an Alien. Try not to become
an Enemy Alien as well,' said my uncle Kurt, himself in
that category.

Most male refugees from Germany had been interned at
the outset of the war. Anti-Nazis, Jews and Nazis alike were
shipped to distant camps in Britain, Canada and the
Australian Outback. In time, the authorities grew more
selective. Anti-Nazis and Jews were brought back and
transferred to the Pioneer Corps, a military unit with a
colourful reputation. In the First World War, it had been a
receptacle for those who, though physically fit, were slow-
witted or undersized. Trusted neither to carry weapons
nor eat with regular cutlery, each was issued with a shovel
and a spoon. I do not know whether the annals of the
Pioneer Corps has been written, but its expansion to
include the new arrivals soon made the Corps one of the
most sophisticated in the British Army. Its cooks were
among the best chefs of Europe and there was no better
place to eat in England then their Officers' Mess. Despite
these temptations I was anxious to partake of active
service. To volunteer for the Polish Army seemed my only
option.

The Polish Embassy was situated in Portland Place, as it
is now, across from the Royal Institute of British Architects,

of which I became a member some years later. I entered the Embassy with my Danzig passport and my identity card from the Polish school. It was Polish policy to regard Danzig as part of its postwar claims, therefore I was considered Polish. The consular official registered me as a volunteer, but as I was underage, told me that some months would elapse before I was called. The delay was unexpected and frustrating. Could an exception be made? Two years ago perhaps, but recruitment into the army, chaotic in the early days, had settled into a routine of regulations.

In the waiting room of the Embassy I encountered the paintings of Felix Topolski for the first time. With taut, swirling lines, he evoked the character of the people he drew and enlivened the scenes with splashes of strong colour. His spontaneity was considered facile by contemporary critics, who would applaud it in Chinese landscape paintings, but failed to appreciate it in Topolski's work. Later, I bought his book *Russia at War*, in which he drew the Poles just released from Soviet labour camps and formed into an army that left for the West. Its soldiers included Menachem Begin, who had still to reach Palestine and make his mark. I was to meet many of these soldiers later, including Begin and, eventually, Felix Topolski.

On returning to Putney, I was able to tell my uncle that, far from being an 'Enemy Alien' to the British authorities, I was about to become a 'Valiant Ally'. 'The Poles will send you into battle barefoot with a pitchfork,' said Kurt, whose opinion of them was not high. He was gifted with the ability of emitting a sarcastic sneeze; on this occasion he sneezed twice.

I realised that I had to find temporary work to support

The central synagogue with a hoarding announcing its destruction, 1938

Interior of the devastated synagogue

With my mother in Danzig

With my father, bound for Lomza

At school in England

With Felix Zarza y Arechavaleta and two unknown ladies at university, 1950

'Can we have our money back if the treaty
signed?' asked an Israeli diplomat when he took o
my works to Camp David, where Begin met S
The drawback of having one's sculptures present
state gifts is that one is seldom at the event. If
receives photographs of the occasion, they are like
be of the President tying his shoelace or a P
Minister hiding one's masterpiece in the shadow
his suit . . .

(Above) Prime Minister Margaret
Thatcher with 'Jerusalem Sphere'

(Right) With Itzhak Rabin at the Knesset,
Jerusalem

(Below) With the Archbishop of
Canterbury, Herzlia, Israel

With Pierre Cardin at the unveiling of the 'Arcadia' sculpture at the 'Peace Forest', Eilat

H.M. King Juan Carlos of Spain with Mr and Mrs Eli Schalit at the presentation of 'Noah's Ark' in Madrid

With US Secretary of Defence Dick Cheney, at an unveiling in Miami

H.M. King Hussein of Jordan, contemplating 'Jerusalem'

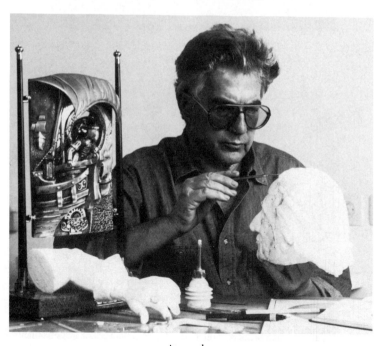

At work

'Torah Shrine', Mannheim, Germany

'Columbus' sculpture, Madrid: *(left)* obverse; *(right)* front

Camels

Bull

Sigmund Freud

myself for a period which, I hoped, would be short.

'God smite Hitler and all his dirty deeds!' said the bishop patriotically and downed the evening's first whisky. 'I've recommended you to a boy's father, told him you can draw. There may be a temporary job for you.' I thanked him and stood, some days later, before an executive table in the offices of a large construction firm. Somewhere a military airport was being built. An assistant Progress-Engineer was urgently needed. 'When could you start?' 'Tomorrow,' I replied. 'Splendid, splendid!' The gentle-man pointed to a small dot on a map of England called Didcot. Others came and went, looked at me discreetly, whispered to each other and left. I felt that there was per-haps a greater sense of urgency and attention than usual paid to such a modest job. I was given papers to sign, received travelling money and an address in Didcot for accommodation. I was there by the weekend.

My room was too large for the small gas fire that attempted to heat it. The gas meter ate pennies and shillings, of which I had few, warming a modest area in which I sat with my feet close to the source. The landlady produced an unaltered diet of baked beans and potatoes, with an egg on Sundays. 'Young men need their starch.' I believe that she confused me with my shirt. I left Didcot in darkness on a workers' bus and in darkness I returned. If Didcot was a town, I never saw it. Stepping out of the bus on my first morning at work, in a harsh wind, I looked for the Progress-Engineer. Someone pointed to a wooden hut in the distance, resembling a railway carriage. No one was in. Piles of rolled up blueprints covered a trestle-table, oth-ers were pinned to boards. A piano stood by the wall and sheets of music were scattered everywhere. 'With your hand on my heart I know we'll never part' was the title on one. Another was called 'The River's Lullaby'.

Men in company duffle-coats opened the door, glanced in and disappeared. A heavy woman came with mugs of tea, stained and lukewarm. For a long time I leafed through back issues of *The Melody Maker*, until I heard a car-door slam. A young man in a long sheepskin jacket rushed in. 'Hello there! You're the new chap. Call me Neil.' I shook hands with the Progress-Engineer. He sat down on top of the blueprints on the table. Swinging his legs, encased in high suede boots, with his flying-clothes, light hair and upturned nose, he looked like an RAF pilot idealised for a recruiting poster. 'I'll be busy all day. Someone will show you around. Wait until Blodwen brings tea. Dreadful stuff, but then, this is Siberia!'

Shrubland and forest had been turned into a wasteland. Felled trees and piles of vegetation rotted at the perimeter. Overhead, ravens circled complaining about the cold or their uprooted nests. In the mud, work crews were preparing the ground for runways which poured out of a fleet of concrete mixers. It was to be my task to record this work on blueprints, and decorate Neil's walls with evidence of progress, leaving him free to play the piano.

On my return to the hut I saw him composing. When there was no pencil between his teeth, the hut echoed to his singing. The score had to be completed quickly so that a ballroom orchestra could play it at the weekend. A band leader would be paid to 'plug' it and it was sure to be a hit. 'Like "Heartbeat by Heartbeat" which took a day to write and netted half a grand.' Neil's head and heart lay in Tin Pan Alley and finally Broadway, where the musical he planned to write would become his crowning glory. 'One lucky note is all it takes and I'm up there with the best of them, old chap! Now be a good fellow and see how those "proles" are getting on. Keep them on their toes!' Turning back to the piano he continued his search for the lucky

152

note. The 'proles' returned the compliment when I appeared before them with my blueprints:

'Where's the ponce then?'

'Don't hear no tinkling piano.'

'Got his self a cushy billet, all beer, 'backy and cock.'

They spoke in a pattern I had to learn, one of repetitive clichés. 'Nice down there?' was the invariable response if one bent down. To someone with a cup of tea: 'Don't drown in it.' Questions were answered as though in self-defence: 'I did, didn't I?' He had it, hadn't he?' Speech was used with reluctance, mainly for light banter or to deflect questions. The rest was silence.

Within a few days I learned that Neil had been exiled by the ultimatum of his father-in-law, a senior director of the construction firm. Didcot, the 'Siberia' that had been chosen, was far enough to keep him out of sight and near enough to bring him back to his wife at weekends in his fast sports car. It also kept him out of the army. My job was to do his job. The company director's daughter came only once. She was dark and stylish in a white fur coat and her visit was short. It had taken Neil, Blodwen and me much longer to clean up, hide the music scores and bury the piano under a pile of charts. Once, a blonde singer arrived to rehearse a duet from 'Blue Birds in London', the musical in which she had been promised the leading role. 'Leaving Siberia for the day, old chap,' Neil would suddenly announce, 'keep an eye on the proles.' The sports car raced towards London and haunts where his father-in-law would never find him.

I walked about, colouring charts in an icy wind. My face was bitten with a painful infection and my fingers and toes were covered in chilblains. 'Piss on them at night,' the workers advised. 'It's the quickest cure.' That seemed to explain the curious smell of the workers' bus in the morning. With urine-covered toes and a throbbing face in a chilly room, my evenings were not happy. Weeks passed, the expanse of concrete grew, Neil's latest scores had to be rushed off to become 'hits' by the weekend. Returning to my room one cold evening, I saw a telegram. The Polish Army wanted me to report for duty. Head office would have to find a new candidate to colour the blueprints.

'I hope you find your lucky note,' I said to Neil when we parted.

'You'll be there at opening night to hear it,' he replied.

Leaving the hut to catch the train to London, piano music accompanied me down the runway until it was drowned by the complaining ravens. In the years ahead I sometimes looked through copies of *The Melody Maker* to see whether Neil had found his lucky note. Perhaps I missed it. All I learned during those three months in 'Siberia' was a sure way to cure chilblains.

To the Bayonets!

I WAS TO SPEND two-and-a-half years in military service. It soon became clear that it was too late for 'glory'. Hope of active service, a 'crack at the Nazis', to use a cliché of the time and revenge for the loss of my parents, faded before the realities I now encountered.

The exiled Polish Government in London had enough fighting men. In addition to those soldiers who had escaped after the collapse of Poland, tens of thousands, whom the Russians had deported to Siberia, had been recently freed and sent to join the army in the West. The government's battles were becoming political, directed at a new enemy and they were destined to lose. The Soviet Union regarded Poland as its 'sphere of interest'. All attempts to invade Russia from the West, in the future as in the past, were likely to come through Poland. The Soviet Government was determined to surround itself with obedient satellite regimes, kept in power by the Red Army. As they defeated the Germans in Poland, they turned from liberators to occupiers, installing a puppet government nominated in Moscow. The Polish Government in London was cut off, never to return to Poland. Neither would most of its soldiers. The Polish Forces were fighting bravely on many fronts but not, it seemed, for the liberation of their country.

While this was happening at the highest political level,

155

at the bottom end three recruits were travelling on a train to Blackpool. Apparently we were the current military intake. A boarding-house many streets from the seafront was our destination. This small hotel, and others like it, were used to accommodate the transients of a Polish military camp on the outskirts of town. We shared a room and, still in civilian clothes, walked about discovering the Tower Ballroom, the Golden Mile, the booths with the Bearded Lady and the Stuffed Mermaid. My fellow recruits had recently graduated from English schools. The father of one was a director of Poland's State Shipping Line, now based in England and knew my parents from earlier times.

Some days later we had a visitor. Senior Sergeant Smigielski, from an airborne unit, short, athletic, with a boxer's nose, had come from Scotland to take charge of us. Over a cup of coffee we heard that he had orders to turn us from recruits into soldiers. This process usually took some months of intensive training, but under the circumstances he believed that two days would do, one tomorrow, the other next week. Meanwhile, he had been told that the Tower Ballroom was not only full of amenable girls, but also famous for its aquarium of saltwater fish. He was interested in both. We could confirm that for the girls from the mill towns, sex on the sand came second only to a sun tan. We had not noticed the fish.

At the Tower over drinks, Sergeant Smigielski described his escape from France at Dunkirk. Following a number of special operations, he had also taken part in the parachute drop on Arnhem. As the Germans knew of it in advance, it had ended in disaster. He had survived the massacre of his unit, crossed through France and over the Pyrenees into Spain. Held there at the infamous Miranda internment camp, he escaped via Portugal, returning to his base in Scotland. On learning of his next assignment – us – he decided that it could be combined with a relaxing week or two at the seaside.

Our training began the following day with a lecture on chains-of-command and a strategic analysis of some historic battles. We then walked to a fairground where he explained the mechanism of a gun before a shooting-booth. We fired at the moving targets but won no prizes. The following week we returned to the booth and watched Sergeant Smigielski win a stuffed toy. It seemed that we had graduated, as he initiated no further training. We saw him occasionally at the ballroom.

I have often wondered whether we had been beneficiaries of Sergeant Smigielski's refined sense of humour or whether he had decided to take his revenge on the army for inflicting him with having to train the likes of us. Evidently he reported his mission accomplished, as we were issued with uniforms and a Sten gun. I kept mine under every bed I slept in for over two years. When I returned it at the end of my service, rusted and coated in blanket fluff, the quartermaster insisted on the price of a bottle of whisky before he would take it back.

A course for Meteorological Observers was about to begin at an RAF College. The Polish Air Force wanted to know the latest techniques in that field and was sending us to acquire them. We were to become instructors on our 'return to Poland'. We received this news from the elderly, grey-faced captain, nominally our commanding officer, when we were called to his office at the camp. Dressed in a silver-braided uniform of bygone days, he sat pensively in a cloud of smoke. There was a cigarette holder between thumb and forefinger, just like the elegant officers I had seen as a child in Kashubia. Our meetings with him were heavy with long silences, during which he stared at us, perhaps in contemplation of happier days, when he would have had us scrubbing floors with a toothbrush, back home, before the world turned upside-down and before he wore dentures that clicked. He would dismiss us with a weary wave of the hand.

I wondered whether to inform the captain that I had no intention of being in Poland after the war. 'Don't be a *freier* (fool),' more experienced soldiers at the boarding-house advised me. 'In the army you take what you get and you get what you take.'

By way of introduction to meteorology, I spent the remaining days at a public library. It appeared to be a somewhat uncertain science, not much advanced from the wisdom of shepherds and sailors. I had learned some of their doggerel at school: 'Red sky at night, shepherds' delight' and 'Mares tails, mares tails, make little ships carry big sails.' But I enjoyed my reading and looked forward to useful work in the war and perhaps beyond.

My evenings were spent in the company of three Polish volunteers from Argentina. Armed with a small accordion and a repertoire of tangos and milongas, they were an enormous hit with the girls on the seafront. During the day they sold black-market clothing coupons and pros- pered. Apart from the basic phrases of seduction, they spoke no English. 'Fancy a little cuddle then?' was direct, but not lacking in finesse. At the Tower Ballroom it would be asked after the third dance and the second drink. A deviation could ruin the enterprise. 'Don't mind if I do,' was the girl's expected response. Any other brought the Argentinians into a huddle on interpretation. Timing was everything and they illustrated it with a tango on their accordion. 'Introduction, slow melodic cruise, tension, confrontation, consummation and *adios*!' At the ballroom the recipe had been honed to a fine routine. I was able to watch practical demonstrations.

158

In this setting the war and the bombs seemed far away. I experienced the flying-bombs only on short visits to London. As a weekend guest in the bishop's home during an air-raid, I had mistaken the nocturnal purring of a cat on my bed for a flying-bomb, droning dangerously above the rooftops. I woke half the household before realising my mistake and was not allowed to forget it in a hurry.

A taciturn man with a pock-marked face and greasy hair was a new arrival at our boarding-house. From his long, nightly walks and tired appearance, I concluded that he was an insomniac. In fact he was one of the couriers between the government in London and the Polish Underground, resting between missions. Before his abrupt departure, he told us about events in occupied Poland. In a level voice, he revealed a glimpse of a horrifying world, of mass starvation, anarchy and death. The left and right factions of the Polish Underground were as active in slaughtering each other as in fighting the Germans. From a distance, he had witnessed a day's routine of extermination at a death camp. We heard in gruesome detail of the smoking chimneys of the crematoria and the sickly-sweet smell of piled-up corpses. Detached and cynical, the courier used the third person when speaking of his experiences. Perhaps it helped him to retain his sanity as he travelled between the carnage in Poland and the corridors of the Polish Government in London.

Numb and enraged, I was unable to accommodate these horrific images into the context of the life I knew. I was certain that my parents could not have survived the inferno he depicted and felt the guilt of being alive, concerned with daily banalities, while they had suffered and died. Like the insomniac courier, I walked for many night hours, finding no answer then, or since.

Most of the boarding-house was occupied by the group of grounded Polish Air Force pilots, whom the Argentinians called '*Los Olvidados*', a word meaning something between forgotten and lost. They had fought against the Germans over Poland and France. Escaping to England with their planes, they took part in the Battle of Britain, flew in ceaseless combat for many months and saw their comrades die in the air. They had helped prevent the German invasion of Britain, wore medals of valour and the faces of old men. Still in their mid-twenties, they were used up. Some were alcoholics, others suffered from nervous ticks or unsteady hands. In the evenings the *olvidados* crowded into the lounge to get drunk. A pianist among them had inserted a sheet of newspaper between hammers and strings, to give the piano a muffled, haunting sound. Their favourite melody was the '*Valse François*', a popular hit before the fall of France. They sang it with the sad passion of old men for the melodies of their youth.

Intensely private, the *olvidados* admitted no one into their circle. It seemed a paradox that the only sociable one among them was the most disfigured, a pilot whose face had been burned into a grotesque distortion of purple flesh. My first sight of him caused an involuntary revulsion which, sadly, he had learned to expect. During his many months in hospital, he had corresponded with a lady in Canada who knew of his condition. His strength came from the hope that they could be happy together. I helped him with his letters and we practised English conversation on walks along the pier. Soon I became so accustomed to his appearance that the horrified stares of passersby would catch me by surprise. On parting, he gave me a photograph of a smiling young pilot, with high cheekbones and light hair. It was the face of a man I had never seen, buried in the purple mask of the man I knew.

On my last night in Blackpool, I went to the Tower Ballroom and danced with a girl from Bradford. A red and blue heart was tattooed on her arm which read 'Arthur'. We walked down to the beach. If our military training had not advanced much, in some matters we had become veterans. To prevent pregnancy, she placed my trouser-belt over my shoulder, and put her leg through it – a familiar ritual of evenings at the seashore. I asked about the name on her tattoo. 'It's all right, luv,' she said, 'when I do it, I think on him.' And so for a short time, under the columns of the pier, I became Arthur. The next morning I left Blackpool.

In the two years that followed I learned and practised meteorology. Cirrus and cumulus clouds, occlusions, cold and warm fronts were my daily routine. I learned to chart and forecast the movement of air that came over Britain en route to the Continent and to assess its suitability for bombing missions over German-occupied Europe.

I was based in Doncaster in the North and in Stanmore in the South. I frequently worked in a subterranean operations centre. Beneath our glass-walled rooms, a large mapping table displayed the changing patterns of air-battles over the channel, the coast and sometimes above our heads. Small plaques with letters and numbers – 'F' for friendly, 'H' for hostile – were moved about with magnetic rods and raked off like chips on a croupier's table.

One tense and busy night the phone rang on my table and a passing colleague picked it up. The caller gave a wicked imitation of a very drunk Winston Churchill demanding the weather report. For good measure he added that he was calling from Chequers, the name of our neighbourhood pub. My colleague shouted abusively at the caller for his ill-timed joke, then drew himself to attention and reeled off the forecast in a shaking voice. The Prime Minister's country residence was also called Chequers and, drunk or not, Winston Churchill was entitled to know.

My work was a cycle of preparing and assessing weather-charts and flights over the Atlantic to gather the information. Flying at night, I could see the bright lights of Ireland from a distance. Their neutrality required no blackout.

Towards the end of my service when the war had ended, I spent a short period photographing the destroyed towns of Holland and Northern Germany from the nose of a Lancaster Bomber. On my first flight, racing low over the Wash and the Channel, I had the sudden feeling that I was returning home. The direction was Danzig. But there could be no return to the past, as I realised when I saw the devastation beneath us. Circling over Cologne, the entire city was a grey, gutted ruin, from which only the spires of the burnt-out cathedral protruded. I wondered how the German people felt. I had last seen them jubilant, their eyes shining, hands outstretched, screaming adoration at their Führer. I saw them now, small figures in the rubble below. Pressing the camera- button over the scene, I could feel no pity. I was recording a just retribution.

I often worked through the night and in the morning, if ground-fog did not cover the countryside, attempted to capture the veils of mist about me with watercolours. An exhibition of eighteenth-century local artists in Doncaster had shown me how suitable the built-up layers of tinted water were for depicting the Yorkshire landscape. Strong shapes in the foreground faded rapidly in the distance and soon vanished into the damp greys of the horizon. It struck me that the English character was in accord with this elusive landscape. The ability to 'make one's hand

come out of other people's sleeves', as the Indian merchant had once described it, is perhaps also best practised
in the fog.

Checking instruments on night-flights and charting the
weather while others slept, brought with it a numbing
detachment. Nights of solitary activity, followed by days of
little sleep, blurred my sense of reality. It was fortunate
that at this point, a small renaissance called Margaret
appeared in my life. Petite, full of energy and intelligence,
she was an attractive brunette, her hair arranged in a careful bun, to fit the Air Force cap. She had come to join the
meteorological team. With a sure eye, she spotted me as an
object in need of renovation, afflicted with intellectual
dilapidation and political dry-rot. She moved in a team of
renovators. Bertrand Russell, Arthur Koestler, Engels,
Gramsci and the poets Auden and MacNeice were among
them. I had to read rapidly and respond with critical com-
ment, which she would demolish with the deft blow of a
judo master. Our forest walks were animated by discus-
sions and her provocative questions. Love-making was like
a series of tea-breaks between seminars. In the three, short
months before she was transferred elsewhere, I had been
altered. The interest in politics and literature which she
had awoken in me, gave me an undeserved reputation
later, at university. We remained in touch over many years,
during which time she went on to Oxford and an eventual
professorship. Sometimes, I look at the photograph of her
face, crowned with its Air Force cap. The challenge in her
eyes and the encouraging jut of her lower lip still force me
to open a self-improving book.

Strolling in a neighbouring forest with my sketch-pad,
one chilly afternoon, I walked into a group of German
soldiers felling trees. Their guard sat dozing on a tree-
stump. I had spoken no German since my grandmother's

death and decided to practise. If I expected to encounter Nazis, I was mistaken. The group were communists to a man. The bright future Hitler had promised them would now come about through world Communism. One had lost some toes in the Russian snow. He took off his boot to show me the gaps. The Germans, with their respect for power, had found it in a new direction – the East. I voiced scepticism after what I had heard of the labour camps and the arbitrary incompetence of the Soviet Union from Polish ex-prisoners in Siberia. '*Na Ja!*' they shouted at me. 'A little *Unteroffizier* like you would not think like us.' Surrounded by a group of tall Germans with axes in their hands, I did not try too hard to win this argument. The absurdity of being in a tight corner with Nazi soldiers for expressing reservations about the Soviet Union struck me only later and from a safe distance.

But at the time I had something else in mind. 'Tell me the words of "Lilli Marlene",' I asked. I had, until then, only heard the song in English. And so, nostalgic for their families, in a forest far from home, those four or five German soldiers recited:

> '*Wie einst Lilli Marlene,*
> *Wie einst Marlen.*'

It seemed the right setting for them – and for me.

Late in 1944, while on leave in London, I had dinner with Heinz, my old friend from the days of Professor Bonelli. He was now called Henry, served in an airborne unit and was full of plans which he intended to carry out once the war ended. Our meal was interrupted when the French cook rushed into the dining-room. In broken English he shouted the news he had just heard over the radio, 'Paris, she has been liberated!' There was no

164

response from the restaurant, except for the clicking knives and forks. For English diners, enthusiasm during a meal was suspect, especially from a Frenchman. Crestfallen, the cook slunk back into the kitchen. My reaction was also muted as I thought of my father. His unbounded faith in France had led him to believe that the French possessed the effective army they claimed and the will to fight. He had been gravely mistaken. Now the Great Wheel had turned and France was back again. For me, too, the wheel was turning. I decided that the time had come to think about life after the war. Within weeks of our dinner, Henry was killed in a training accident.

My eventual release from the army came with an unexpected and welcome scholarship to study 'any subject, anywhere in England'. It was the result of an examination set by the Polish Government months before, to select a cadre of potential 'intellectuals' for postwar Poland. The government was disintegrating and this must have been a considerable strain on its remaining financial resources. I have good reason to be grateful for it. The news that I had been selected reached me when I returned to base, sore, coughing and scratching my skin, after ten days at a military experimental station on Salisbury Plain. Bravado and a desire to rid myself of the chronic aversion to blood which I had inherited from my father, had led me to answer the appeal for volunteers. With other human guinea pigs, I had been confined in gas chambers with exploding canisters of the newly invented DDT, mustard gas and mosquitoes. The combination of lung, skin and malarial problems which could have spiced our later life, did not occur to me, and fortunately never happened. Between experiments, I rented a horse from a local farmer and rode over the shrubland, far away now from Arthur

Levandowski's baleful criticism of my deportment. Arthur would, however, have enjoyed the sight of me galloping into a well-disguised marsh, where shoulder-deep in floating vegetation, I spent a tense hour disentangling the hysterical horse and myself. There had been no marshes in Danzig to practise in.

I reported to a Polish military camp near Lincoln, with the scholarship recipients. We were told that the British authorities had to be kept in absolute ignorance of this project. Therefore our release was an unofficial leave of absence dependent on finding a university that accepted us immediately. Should funds run out in the future, we would at least have had an academic start. Neither food ration cards nor other necessities of civilian life could be issued to us and we had to appear at camp every pay-day when the English paymasters came. For a long time I took the train to Lincoln twice a month, arriving at the base to stamp my feet and shout out my army number at them. The paymasters looked suspiciously at the crowd of foreigners, who were apparently 'up to something' and pretended not to speak English. They could smell a rat but did not know where it was buried. Two barracks along, I handed the money back to a Polish paymaster and returned to university in the evening. On my first day at the camp, I ran into two of the Argentinians from Blackpool; the third was in jail. They were awaiting his release before returning to Buenos Aires. The accordion still intact, we celebrated our reunion and toasted the girls of Blackpool.

The camp was crowded with soldiers who came and went. Those with families in Poland had little choice but to return home and take their chance with Communism. Others chose to remain or emigrated to the United States. I turned down an offer to be part of a gang specialising in car theft, with the excuse that I couldn't drive. 'We'll drive,' they said, 'but we need someone who speaks English to sell them.' I heard that the gang did well before emigrating to Canada.

I was involved in fights on two occasions. Once when a soldier praised Hitler for killing the Jews. Following a punch-up, we spent the night under arrest, in separate cells. On the second occasion I was in the cafeteria of Lincoln Station, where a dapper Englishman, to impress his girl, was being monotonously insulting about Poles. A story had circulated far and wide about an over-passionate Pole who had bitten off his English girlfriend's nipple. Though I felt no responsibility for this, nor for the Polish Army in general, I was wearing the uniform and the tirade was aimed at me. I had learned long ago from Bubi that if one hits hard enough, one blow will suffice. I attempted it amid spilled tea-cups. A policeman was called and noted down details but I heard no more about it. It was a hasty response, which I regretted at leisure on the long train journey back to university. After all, I was supposed to be an 'intellectual' now and, as such, my blows were meant to be of the mind and not of the fist.

With a portfolio under my arm, I travelled to Cambridge, Newcastle and Liverpool. In it were my evocations of the mists of Yorkshire, the 'grand' perspective vistas of Harrow on the Hill and memories of Danzig. To give my appearance a touch of class, Kurt had loaned me a dark suit, which I wore despite reservations each time I caught sight of myself in a mirror. I was accepted at Emmanuel College, Cambridge and by the faculties of the other universities. However their policy was first to admit their own ex-students returning from military service. My own studies could only begin in the following academic year. I was unable to explain my reasons for urgency, in case the British authorities came to hear of them.

Manchester and Trinity College, Dublin, were next on the list. At the former, Kurt had prepared the ground by contacting a friend at the university and I was to be her house-guest. She owned a fine collection of modern art, including the works of Lowry, who was then little known outside Manchester. I was fascinated by the large canvasses of urban scenes in which grey, bent figures walked through desolate streets. It occurred to me that I might soon be among them.

Next morning I was interviewed by the Professor of Architecture. A classical scholar, his room was decorated with the models and drawings of Greek Temples. He was a diminutive man, a halo of white hair encircling his head. With his benign smile, shrewd eyes and posy in his button-hole, he resembled an Irish leprechaun. I was to see a great deal of him in the years to come, as well as his dou-ble in the cinema, the actor Barry Fitzgerald. As with a leprechaun, my meeting with him brought luck. He ad-mitted me at once. An hour later, I had an official letter of acceptance. I walked out through a campus of tall, Victorian-Gothic buildings. A black meteor stood upright in the quadrangle, as though hurled down from outer space as an endorsement of the claim that 'what Manchester thinks today, London does tomorrow.'

In a light, drizzling rain, I went on to explore the Lowry landscape. It was not hard to find. Part of Manchester's city centre had been levelled by bombs. I walked along vast stretches of gutted buildings, soot-encrusted brick walls, tall gas towers, rail junctions, a polluted waterway and smoking factory chimneys. The term 'Industrial Revolution' had, until now, only been an abstract history lesson to me. Here I saw its reality. Compared with

London, the people looked pale, undersized, their clothes as drab as the buildings. I was struck by the number of drunks, the deformed and those suffering from congenital syphilis. 'Illuminated factories with more windows than Italian palaces, smoking chimneys, taller than Egyptian obelisks,' Disraeli had written of it a century before and it had not changed. In time I came to see a strange beauty in this ugliness, like the revelation of a truth stripped of all pretence. But by then I too wore a drab, over-large rain-coat, heavy shoes against the rising damp, had become pale, and snivelled with sinusitis. Just another figure in a Lowry painting.

To celebrate my undergraduate status and reciprocate the hospitality of my hostess, I invited her to dinner. As the week of travelling had depleted my money, I decided that the time had come to sacrifice the suit. Kurt was shorter than me, the trousers were too wide, the jacket heavily padded about the shoulders. No doubt it had been the latest fashion in Bavaria a generation ago, but I had the distinct awareness of raised eyebrows when I wore it in Cambridge. I found a second-hand clothes shop, with the large notice, 'Why shiver? – We must sell!', walked in and put the suit on the counter. The man fingered it. 'Nice bit of cloth,' he said, 'pity it's made for a hunchback. Give you eighteen bob.' 'It's not,' I said, 'and if it were you'd have no trouble finding hunchbacks here.' 'For *chutzpah*, I'll throw in another two bob.' 'I want five.' 'That's not *chutzpah*, that's gall.' I took the extra two shillings and hoped that Kurt would not want his suit back. That too, I suppose, was *chutzpah*, if not gall.

My hostess came with her lover, a trawler-skipper half her age. Over dinner they invited me to join them on a trip into the Irish Sea. On the following day, I sat at the prow of the trawler. It was bright, cold and the waves were rough. Porpoises dived in the vicinity and a swarm of sea-gulls converged on the nets and on the fish that the crew were gutting. I spoke in German to the water. 'What you wanted, I've done,' I said to my father. 'From now on I'll have to take my own advice – wish me luck!' I was twenty years old and had made it to university.

It seemed fitting that my military career should end as unconventionally as it had begun. I had almost graduated from university four years later when I returned to my digs one evening and found a small package on the hall table. It contained the information that my military service was over, notice of a promotion and a medal. I left it there and a few days later it had vanished, like the Polish Government.

On a motorway near London there is a sign pointing towards a Polish Air Force memorial. I have never been there, but hope that it pays fitting tribute to the young pilots who fought so bravely, many of whom were killed, and some fortunate to survive with their memories and the sad melody of the *'Valse François'*.

'You'll Never Get to Heaven
as an Architect'

ARCHITECTURE seemed to be the right discipline in which to combine my possible talent in art with the university degree I had promised my father. Time would tell if the choice was right.

My first task in Manchester was to find accommodation. The university sent me to see a vacancy at the Unitarian Theological College, situated in a large Victorian house. I was shown into a stark, whitewashed room with a sagging metal bed, as though generations of theological students had wrestled there with the Trinity. Though younger than the theologians, they treated me with respect, perhaps because of the vestiges of uniform I wore. Without clothing coupons and little money, I was still in battledress and army boots, lightened by baggy corduroy pants won at a poker game at the air-base. In the evening the students questioned me on points of Jewish religion and I did not know most of the answers. To my great embarrassment, they had learned more about Judaism than me. Sneaking into the college library for a source of information, I found Noth's *History of the Jews* and began to read.

Though written off as theologically useless, there must have been something rakish about my appearance because within a week a delegation of scholars came to my door to enquire about the Facts of Life. It took time before I realised that they were in earnest. I understood that their

171

concern was with marital duties, not the rough and ready activities I had been taught in Blackpool. Using my best architectural technique, I drew cross-sections of Adam and Eve, restricting myself to the missionary position as most appropriate to their careers. A week later, I was asked to leave, ostensibly because I had no ration card to contribute to the housekeeping. I hoped that the exchange of information, a history of the Jews for a short course on procreation, had been mutually beneficial.

Fortunately the landlord of my second 'digs' was also the manager of a grocery shop. Ration cards were a mere bagatelle to him. In my new, small room, I set up my drawing-board. A cupboard and chair took up the remaining space. At times, when I had to build an architectural model, the cardboard sheets and balsa wood so crowded the room, that it was simpler to sleep on my neighbour's floor. The view through the window was designed for a budding architect; the close-up of a brick wall.

I stayed there, content and in good company, for over three years. The grocer's wife, a wonderful Yorkshire woman, worked from morning to night for her boarders and baked bread when everyone was asleep. A spacious kitchen with a large, scrubbed table was the centre of the house. Around it we ate, joked, argued, often played poker through the night and knew that we had a home. Danzig apart, when I think of where I come from it's from that kitchen and the North Country warmth I felt there.

My studies had begun. During a visit to London, my aunts presented me with a glossy book on the Modern Movement in Architecture. With that and some sharpened pencils, I joined forty students in a crowded work-studio. There could not have been a better time to enter the profession. The war had caused massive destruction throughout the world and for half a decade all building had ceased. A vast desolation lay waiting to be rebuilt by new planners and builders, as well as technical and aesthetic innovators. The romantic heroes of the next decades in the weekly stories of *Woman's Own* were to be mainly architects, instead of the usual doctors and lawyers. From office girls to social thinkers, everyone was dreaming about us.

But our assembled group would have been a grave disappointment to the readers. Most of us had been in the war, some were in balding middle-age, married with children. For these, it was too late for undergraduate bonhomie, late-night drinking and debates on Existentialism. Wives and nappies were waiting for them in crowded rooms, qualifications had to be acquired without delay. It was not an atmosphere conducive to social and aesthetic vision. All were anxious to catch up on lost time, rush through exams and make a living. Postwar architecture is in part the reinforced-concrete expression of that urgency. 'The only movement in which I have an interest,' a naval officer said with a cynical grin, as he leafed through my glossy book, 'is the movement of money into my pocket.' He was expressing the *Zeitgeist*.

A jarring note marred our first day. In velvet suit and silk cravat, a tutor came to deliver an introductory chat. Long-haired, hand on hip, he concluded his discourse with the recommendation that in order to produce good architecture, we could do worse than marry rich women. I was too shy to ask whether his wife had a sister. Chauvinistically male, militantly left or married to women who were not rich, the audience dismissed him with contempt and he was not seen again. It is possible, however, that had his advice been taken more seriously, a generation of gentlemen-architects, rather than municipal council hacks, would have made postwar architecture look a little better.

173

Each of us spent the first months in the studio stretch-
ing a large sheet of wet and expensive paper over the
drawing board. When it dried to become taut as a drum,
we meticulously copied details of Greek and Roman architecture onto it. Countless washes of Chinese ink were
required to shade Corinthian columns, pediments, 'egg
and dart' ornament, writhing Centaurs and the Sabine
Women in the process of being raped. 'Classical landscape
with Figures' was the title of our effort.

It was the last we saw of that tradition, a sentimental left-
over from a time when the knowledge of classical detail
was the better half of architecture. Thereafter we were
taught to create another environment, in the style of the
great French guru Le Corbusier. His vision of the New
World was one of 'vertical cities', built of crude concrete,
free from the constraints of traditional materials. Under
the guidance of his many books and manifestos, faced with
a challenge of massive, low-budget housing programmes,
we saw ourselves as potters at a giant wheel, creating new
shapes for humanity. When it finally acquired a name it
was 'Neo-Brutalism'. It seemed that the only use for the
past was to grind it up for the concrete-mixer. From
Corbusier's writings we had learned his clichés: 'A house is
a machine for living in' and 'Burn what you love, love what
you burn'. And so we burned up the old and ended up
being burnt by the new.

Despite his enormous influence, Corbusier, the ex-
Cubist and sometime Fascist under Vichy, built very little.
His disciples worldwide made up for that by building too
much. Years later I visited the concrete metropolis, erected
in the spirit of his teaching, in the Brazilian jungle, the
country's capital Brasilia. It is laid out in the shape of a
gigantic aeroplane, symbolic perhaps of the inhabitants'
desire to spend as little time there as possible. I walked

among the huge, grey, identical tower-blocks that housed the government ministries. There was little natural protection from the heat. The architects and planners wanted no foliage to spoil the effect of the concrete jungle. I wandered along miles of cement, cracked walls, the huge inverted pyramid that is the stadium for the masses and the gigantic concrete bubble that is their cathedral. Attempting to leave the city on a Friday, a stampede of bureaucrats raced past me to climb onto the waiting planes, while arriving aircraft disgorged a herd of call-girls, come to console those unlucky enough to be stranded in Brasilia over the weekend. 'Only our pens are here, Senhor,' said the Brazilian official at my side as we circled the city and flew towards Rio, 'our vital parts are elsewhere.' For character and vivacity, Brasilia fell far short of the nearby shanty-town, not shown on any map, where construction workers and their women, now unemployed, lived, played and hired themselves out as servants in the city.

To view the results of postwar architecture, most city centres will suffice. I recall the solemn pilgrimage of our class to London to study the master plan of the reconstruction of the bombed areas around St Paul's Cathedral. The foremost architects and planners explained their concept to the students who listened with deference. Their projects were built and they were rewarded with knighthoods. It is now accepted that the area cannot be pulled down fast enough. It required more affluent economic times, a hard second look and a new name, Post-Modernism, to improve on the drab world we were taught to build.

Between drawing-board and lecture room, the first year soon passed. My fellow boarders around the dining table at night were three Lebanese, a Yugoslav recently come

On the Vistula Facing East

from Tito's partisans and forever searching for hidden microphones, and a Welsh-speaking Basque called Felix Zarza y Arechavaleta. Son of a minister in the Spanish Republican Government, he had been evacuated to Wales during the war and was nicely seduced there by his foster mother. Short, barrel-chested, a pocket-size version of Anthony Quinn, he was dedicated to the seduction of tall women, without neglecting the short ones on the way. The innate talent of a Don Juan combined with the poetic inflections of a Welsh accent made him irresistible to both kinds. His style was closely studied by imitators such as I. Apart from that we also became friends.

We had both been separated early from our families. Our achievement had been the ability to adapt. The price for it was a large measure of detachment from whatever life would confront us with thereafter. Although from opposite sides of Europe, we recognised that similarity and, without speaking of it, it created a bond that has continued through the years.

Commercial travellers came and went with their samples and jokes. Two teachers from Manchester Grammar School were regulars, as was a Labour leader, whose monthly circuit included visits to Manchester and evenings with us at the pub. At dinnertime the landlady brought her aged father from his room, said 'Cumun our dad, seat thy sel' here' and placed him at the head of the table. Tall and gaunt, like an old eagle, his eyes darted about in wonder at the strangers in his daughter's home. The landlord's cousin, on occasional leave from Strangeways prison, showed us how to speak without moving one's lips and split a match into four functioning parts; useful knowledge in case we ever followed in his footsteps in this uncertain world.

Dinner debates, arguments and card games lasted well

into the night. Guests arrived and joined in. Sometimes we tried to smuggle girls into our rooms. When we succeeded it was because our landlady thought it might do us good before our exams, which it did. Like most of the Arab students, the Lebanese differed from us in their affluence, which enabled them to indulge in their favourite women, hefty peroxide blondes. Among the first words of Arabic I learnt was *Hafla* – a celebration, which they occasionally held in a suite at the Midland Hotel. I was sometimes invited. They danced singly to hand-clapping and a clay drum, while the girls who nibbled the pistachio nuts and baklava, sat, watched and waited for their turn in the bedroom. 'You a wog then, like t'uthers?' asked my blonde companion suspiciously when one of the Arabs introduced me as his brother. I nodded gravely, afraid that I might not otherwise be part of the package-deal, called out *Inshallah* at the critical moment and tried to keep silent for the rest of the time.

Lacking the budget of an Arabian prince, I found the study of architecture costly. My allowance from the Polish authorities had been adequate, but the Polish administration had faded away and their obligation was assumed by a British ministry. The transfer expressed itself in a drastic cut in our monthly cheque. A clerk somewhere in London appeared eager for us to fail an exam so that he could permanently remove us from the national budget. Handmade paper, paints, colours, drafting tools and the materials for architectural models mounted in expense as our studies progressed. These things could be purchased in various places in town, but it was advisable to buy them only in the little shop of Mr Scofield, the caretaker. Though more expensive, they were nevertheless a wise investment, for if knowledge is power, 'Lofty' Scofield was a powerful man.

177

Bony and tall, he carried himself erect, as befits a Sergeant-Major, even in retirement. A lifetime of out-witting his superiors from Cheltenham Barracks to the Hindu Kush had given Mr Scofield's sharp face a deferential smile, belied by calculating eyes. Retired now, he wore braces over a heavy vest, left his dentures soaking in a jam-jar at his side, and waited for us to buy his goods. With the professional talent of a Company Sergeant-Major, Lofty knew everything that had been said, was done, or about to happen, within the walls of our school. It was understood that we purchased that information together with our drawing materials. No sooner were the exams over than one could knock on his door at night. He would open it just enough to hiss 'yer paased!' or the dreaded 'yer faaled!' and shut it in our faces. As his index fingers typed out the official results, it was rumoured that these frequently depended on the quantity of drawing material one purchased, and the state of one's account with him.

Armed with Mr Scofield's advance knowledge I was able to plan the summer holidays. For the first two months I usually worked in a steam-pit, where African logs lay boiling till they were ready to be peeled into plywood. The factory in Trafford Park used Irish labourers, recently arrived and hoping to head for London. No one wanted to boil alongside the logs for too long. My plans were similar. After paying Mr Scofield's bills, sufficient remained to pack a rucksack and head for the motorway that led to London and the South. I did not need Chairman Mao to tell me that a journey around the world started with an outstretched arm.

Weeks later, in St Paul de Vence, Ronda or sipping mint tea in Tangiers, I would warm myself in the Mediterranean sun. Memories linger, but a suntan fades fast in Manchester and sinusitis was just around the corner.

Returning to my place in the work-studio, the muse that inspires architects was tapping her fingernails on my drawing-board. 'You are late, another year began five minutes ago!'

To recognise an architect at a party, look for the person who can find his own way to the toilet. Architecture is a profession which soon leaves its mark on those who study it and we were becoming professional. The most crucial of the subjects we learned is also the one most taken for granted. Architecture is judged by its appearance but, whether beautiful or ugly, one expects its component parts to function. Structure must hold up, liquid flow through pipes and when the finger touches a switch there must be light. All of this was taught to us as 'building construction' and the evolution of building construction is the history of architecture. We learned that behind the grand architectural concept, an infinity of parts had to be created and put in their place. 'God is in the detail', we were taught and, as in the Great Universe, so in the little world of the architect nothing must be left to chance. It was a discipline which soon ingrained itself into our character. 'The architect will detail the elopement while the builder carries off the bride', was another less flattering definition, and true at least in the financial sense.

This training caused a major adjustment problem, when years later I turned to another branch of the arts. God may well reside in the detail for an architect but in other fields that is generally where the devil lurks; there to over-labour a detail can be as dangerous as to under-design it in architecture. From Leonardo da Vinci to Jackson Pollock, artists know that the viewer's imagination responds to the implied rather than to the explicit. Pleasure, like fear, is more acute where the details are left undefined. It was

179

with difficulty that I learned to retreat from what is so essential in architecture but superfluous elsewhere. Old habits die hard. With each sculpture I start, a new battle commences. In my head, an architect in a three-piece suit wrestles with a bearded stranger in sandals. As they gouge and kick each other, my sculpture takes shape. I hope that neither will ever win, or else I will lose my job as referee.

But these problems were still ahead. The immediate one was to complete our design projects in time for the Friday night 'hop' at the Students' Union and to carry off a bride without the help of the builder.

Nonchalance should not be practised in an ill-lit room. I made that discovery when my sleeve caught fire on an open candle flame. The arm I had so elegantly extended spilled its jug of lager over an attractive girl. In our mutual rush for the water tap, we collided and fell. With one elbow on the linoleum and her skirt high above her knees, my victim managed a dignified bow, extended a petite hand and said, *'enchantée'*.

Thus, on the kitchen floor, at a party, I met Odette. She came from Alsace. Our acquaintance might have been ordained by higher powers. Odette's education had been from the nuns of Nôtre Dame de Zion. Nightly, she had joined them in their prayer for the conversion of the 'perfidious Jews'. I was her first living example. With Odette still wet and my sleeve still smouldering, we spoke about Camus and her longing for a glass of Pernod. Hearing that her birthday was near, I promised to compensate her with a whole bottle. Two weeks later we drank it together in a small hotel in Grasmere and made love. I realised that it was her first time. *'Je fais des bêtises,'* she whispered. I hoped that events would prove her wrong. It was Easter in my fourth year at Manchester, and I had never been happier.

Grasmere in the Lake District is Wordsworth country and
the reason which had brought Odette to England.
Invisible but always present on our walks was William
Wordsworth. He had lived and died in the Lake District,
but his early and formative years were spent in France. A
disciple of Voltaire and Rousseau, he had narrowly
escaped the guillotine during the Revolution. Odette's thesis dealt with the influence of French poetry on his work.

> And I can listen to thee yet;
> Can lie upon the plain
> And listen, till I do beget
> That golden time again.

Hearing her recite his poetry in French translation, it
seemed as if this thoroughly English poet in this English
landscape of hills and lakes we walked through, had been
transposed to the other side of the Channel.

I had acquired a larger room in Manchester. In addition
to a view of the garden there was the constant trickle of a
brook which meandered across the lawn. Too long in town
for illusion, I regarded it as an open drain. But the water
was clear and as it disappeared into neighbouring property
the quacking of ducks there seemed to confirm its status.
On weekends, Odette left the student's hostel and stayed
with me. With great charm and in imitation of Wordsworth, she composed the only poem I have ever received,
'Ode to an Open Drain'. Together with the aroma of
Gaulloise cigarettes, she permeated the room with sentiment, passion and moments of startling practical shrewd-
ness. Perhaps these were Gallic qualities. I enjoyed
anticipating them in our months together. I learned that
she had lost her father early, had a brother at university
and lived with her mother. Her uncle was a bishop of some

importance in the French hierarchy and head of the family. The Sisters of Nôtre Dame de Zion had been his choice for her education.

By the summer, Odette's research in England was at an end. Wordsworth's French influence had been established and bound into a handsome volume. I added illustrations of the Lake District to it. We planned to spend some days in Paris and a week in the Vosges mountains near her home. A bachelor uncle had recently died there and his house and fields were passing to her family. There, in the company of her brother, we would spend our week.

After six beautiful and lazy days in Paris and a long train journey, we stood before Odette's home. It was a large stone house with a formal garden. An elegant staircase led up to the front door. I met Odette's mother just before dinner. Two servants came and went with food when she rang her bell. 'I confess to not being overly fond of Jews, Monsieur. They pry into one's affairs,' said Odette's mother, conversationally as she poured the wine. 'Perhaps we like to know which way the wind is blowing,' I replied, 'as a matter of survival.' The subject changed, but I had felt the wind and knew how it blew. After dinner I was given a tour of the gardens and orchard. Passing little mounds of rotting leaves, Odette's mother turned them over with her cane to reveal hundreds of grazing snails. 'Pity you must go,' she said, 'by the weekend they will make a delicious soup.' I mumbled regrets, thanked my lucky stars and expressed gratitude for her hospitality. We were to leave early in the morning.

Next day we headed for the Vosges to join Odette's brother, François and his fiancée. The train took us to a small, hilly town that had changed its name many times over the centuries from French to German and back again. The uncle's house was narrow and steep. A stone sink in the living room served as kitchen and bathroom. The toilet was a hole beneath the stone stairs and appeared to discharge into a bottomless pit below. Fine marble columns and a well-stocked wine cellar were in odd contrast to this starkness. A stone plaque showed a date from the seventeenth century.

French families appear to enjoy the litigation that comes with inheritance. Other relatives were waiting in the wings to dispute the uncle's will. Before a fight, however, it helps to know what there is to quarrel about. A notary arrived with documents, like a figure from a Daumier cartoon. Over a bottle of Mirabelle brandy he suggested that I was best qualified to locate the fields on maps at the municipal hall. He would obtain the necessary permit in a day or two. *'Au revoir maître – à bientot monsieur l'architecte.'*

On the appointed day, I sat in the *mairie*, the little municipal hall. Crossed Tricolour flags decorated the wall behind an empty desk. On other walls, with impressive impartiality, hung pictures of French and German generals, with dedications that thanked the citizens of the town for their loyalty and cooperation. They dated back to the campaigns of Napoleon and finished, for the moment at least, with the Second World War. A pile of massive black ledgers was placed on the table before me. Inside, the maps had faded. A surveyor's hand from the time of Napoleon had drawn a grid of rectangles over hill and dale. Each was a field, its name inscribed with an elegant flourish, 'Hog's Path', 'Evil Creek', 'The Kingdom of Heaven right at the Top'. I checked them against a list the notary had prepared and located those belonging to the uncle.

Next morning we set out with a picnic basket to inspect the properties. We climbed over hilly terrain on a sunny August day, cut through green meadows and jumped from

183

rock to rock to cross the brooks. At noon we picnicked in one of the uncle's fields and then walked on to locate another. A large shed stood on the border beside a dilapidated path. We tried the keys François had found on a ring in the house. The door opened reluctantly.

We walked into a stench of mould, mixed with the smell of leather. German army boots stood before us in rows. Neat stacks of cut-out leather on work-benches awaited completion. A calendar distorted by damp hung frozen in time. The year it showed was 1943. In Auschwitz the chimneys were still smoking and my parents had just been murdered. The blades were rusting on the cutting machines. The last delivery truck had never come. Boots waited by the door, in military rows, ready to march. I thought of the sound they made on the streets and of those that had listened to it from their hiding places. We walked out in silence and inspected no more properties.

I left a few days later. Odette embraced me before I boarded the night train to Paris. We had made plans to be together for Christmas. She ran off before the train left, so that I would not see her cry. On the train journey, I was attacked by an intestinal infection, probably caused by the wet ground on which we had picnicked. I spent the hours being sick, while the conductor called out the names of the stations through the night, '*Chaumont, Chaumont, tous les passagers à destination de Paris . . .*' I arrived in Paris at dawn. With difficulty, I reached the hotel we had stayed in two weeks before and lay there for some days, shaking with fever. Back in Manchester, I lived on boiled rice for a long time.

There had also been a disturbance in Alsace. The bishop was informed that his niece had compromised her virtue and, moreover, the villain was a Jew. The wrath of God had descended on the family for permitting Odette to reside in a land of heretics. The few letters I received from her sounded reticent and sad. I waited for our Christmas meeting in Paris and for a letter informing me of her plans. Instead I received an invitation to her wedding. It was decorated with an episcopal coat of arms. A second invitation arrived the following day, as though His Grace wanted to stress the point. Apparently the groom resided in Basel. Odette had never mentioned him. The introduction must have been effected quickly and conclusively. Some months later, a package came from Odette. It contained a letter and a book of Rilke's poems. I read her first sentence only: 'Forgive me my friend, I know that you are hurt.' I folded the letter into the book and never opened either again. She was right; a great sadness hurts, but words are not the cure.

The year passed and friends who studied other subjects graduated and disappeared. Both their absence and their letters made me restless. The Yorkshire landlady left her husband for one of the teachers at the Manchester Grammar School. I found temporary digs elsewhere in the neighbourhood; it emphasised the disintegration of what had almost been my family. Manchester seemed a colder place which I, too, intended to leave when the year was over.

At the university, our concern was with the final thesis, the grand opus which would determine our graduation. Everyone searched for a suitable subject. I asked my professor whether mine could be a proposal for the Edinburgh Festival Building. The yearly art festival was then coming into vogue. With his blessing I travelled to Edinburgh, saw the dramatic beauty of the city and spoke with officials there about the scope of my undertaking. I returned to my drawing-board in Manchester and prepared plans, perspectives and a model of my Edinburgh project. We also had to work hard on a dozen final exams for our new profession. When they were over, I went to see Mr Scofield for the last time. Lofty's red nose and concave mouth confronted me through a slit in the door, 'Yer paased!' Before he could slam it in my face, I wedged my foot in the door. 'Thank you for everything, Mr Scofield. The next exam I'll attend will be my post mortem.' His mouth opened in a silent laugh, displaying all his gums. 'Don't knock at my door then, 'cause yer'll pass that too.' The door slammed.

Our theses were displayed on the walls of the faculty building, where cubicles had been temporarily erected. Architects had come from various parts of the country as a panel to assess our work. Their stately progress was monitored and reported while we awaited their approach. They had gone to lunch, we were told. Our professor, their host, would ply them with good wine to make the rest of their visit brief and happy. In the late afternoon the group stood before my work. I saw no sign of brevity or happiness. One of the professors was a no-nonsense Scot in a rough textured suit. Another wore a Bohemian cloak and beret. A third, slim, tall and elegantly-dressed, had a London air about him. They lingered, pointed, whispered, made notes and moved on. It was all over! A passing colleague handed me a bottle of brandy. I was in the middle of a large gulp when the tall man with a London air reappeared. 'Nice solution, liked the work. Have something in mind for you in London. Do nothing till you hear from me.' I nodded silently and swallowed the brandy still in my mouth.

It seemed that I had passed and had a job in London all at the same time. The brandy must have been taking effect, because all about me I heard a loud, resounding

Hallelujah chorus. Through the windows I could see a sunny evening. Next day would be sunny too and full of promise, just like the weeks and months to come. That night I celebrated at the Cosmo Club. A jazz group belted out hot rhythm, black American soldiers danced with the brown girls who worked there for Benny, the owner. I woke up in a strange bed next to one of Benny's brown girls, a graduation present from the Cosmo Club.

I waited for weeks for the promised call, but it never came. Somewhere in my mind there is a cubicle in which I still sit with my drawings, waiting as agreed, till I hear from the important man. The rest of me marched on long ago.

'Over and Out'

U NDER THE COLONNADES, the little band played
'Domino, Domino' again and again, under instructions from Texan honeymooners. They danced to it across
the Piazza San Marco in Country and Western style. A
dream hatched in Dallas was coming true before my eyes.
A swarm of pigeons rose and fell in response to handfuls
of corn. During the war, their number had been much
reduced by hungry Venetians. It was time now to grow fat
again and multiply.

I sat in the Café Florian, watching the light fade in the
piazza. The pigeons rose like a cloud and disappeared for
the night. Napoleon had called the piazza the most elegant
drawing-room in Europe. I raised my glass to toast a fly on
the table; for it was to fly-shit that I owed my presence
there.

The discovery of the patterns it made on the tired slides
illustrating the *History of Architecture* had been fortunate. In
a soporific monotone, our professor, the genial leprechaun, taught the subject in a room filled with stale air and
dozing students. The slides clicked in the dark, projecting
a succession of Greek temples. The names of their gods
had been long forgotten. Known now only in alphabetical
order, grey and fuzzy, all appeared alike in their detail and
the boredom they generated. It was then that I noticed
dots of fly-shit on the slide of Temple B and their resem-

188

blance to a Picasso profile. Temple C came with a daisy pattern, while the next one showed a crack in the glass resembling a mouth with two beady eyes, the features perhaps of an Olympian god. Now that I was suddenly able to tell the temples apart and to keep awake, I began to ask questions about them. The leprechaun mistook this for an interest in the Classics and as a classical scholar himself, thought kindly of me from then on.

I had graduated, but remained in Manchester working for the City Architect, to pay off a debt to my uncle and accumulate a little money towards a future still uncertain, in a location still unknown. A request from my professor to meet him in his office came as a surprise. He informed me that the Mayor of Venice had invited schools of architecture throughout the world to each send a recent graduate to a conference. Recalling my interest in nameless temples, he had decided to dispatch me with a small allowance to represent our university. The subject was the postwar direction the city should take. Young minds would gather in Venice to solve ancient problems.

Some weeks later I sat in a train heading south. Like me, some two hundred architects were converging on Venice from distant places like Finland, Chile, Moscow and Australia, to determine the New Look of the Serenissima Republica. I imagined the Doges turning in their graves, but know now that they could only have been smiling. Venetian bureaucracy had known for a thousand years how to make unwanted documents rot away in its archives.

When the train passed over the long, narrow causeway connecting Venice to the mainland, I saw the city in the afternoon sun and realised that neither I nor two hundred like me would make the slightest impact here. The Mayor, in his Byzantine wisdom, had more likely called this conference so that Venice would leave its mark on us.

At the railway station I was met by a dark girl in a chic uniform, with a large conference badge. She walked me to a little hotel. I was to share a room there with the Cuban delegate who had yet to arrive. My guide presented me with a badge of my own and tickets to the plays and concerts of the coming Arts Festival, the museums and the Biennale. The Mayor expected us at a reception in the Municipal Palace on the following day. Work would commence thereafter. She regretted that she was otherwise engaged and could not accept my invitation to dinner, smiled seductively in the direction of two elegant Venetians with dark glasses, and darted towards them to have her hand kissed.

I unpacked and went in search of the Piazza San Marco in time for the sunset. '*Sempre diritto, signore.*' The waves of the lagoon made puddles along the piazzetta. I waded through them as I had done so often on the quays of Danzig. I knew that it was time to take the next step in my life and that the decision would come before I left the city. I strolled towards the little band that played 'Domino', waved at the Texan couple, sat down, ordered a drink and waited for the fly.

That night I also discovered that my room was situated above the municipal fire-station, whose red motorboats tested their engines in continuous relays. Throughout my stay in Venice, when I could sleep at all, their roar became incorporated into my dreams and to this day whenever that city is mentioned, engines roar in my head.

Within days we were divided into language groups: Italian, English, French and Spanish. Lectures were given on the problems of the city, the encroaching waters, the relocation of industry and the integration of the new with the old. It soon became apparent that a great divide separated the Gallic from the Anglo-Saxon mind. While

190

the French delegation grew poetic about the optical qualities of shimmering canals and the buildings they reflected,
the English were measuring the railway tracks with
callipers. The French soared into space, while the Anglo-
Saxons descended into the drainage system to tap on
pipes. Americans preferred 'little ole Europe' the way it
was. The Germans were too traumatised by defeat to be
assertive. Latin Americans gathered in little piazzas to
argue politics and sing to their guitars.

Venice was crowded with talent that year. The finest
actors, directors, musicians and painters had come to per-
form at the Fenice, exhibit at the Biennale or simply to
share in the postwar euphoria that held out so much
promise. An impressive assembly of architects had also
arrived to lecture and lead our work-groups. With the
innate good taste of their country, the Italians among them
would break away from the grey brutality of concrete into
a more imaginative Neo-Romantic style of architecture. Of
these, Franco Albini offered me work in his Milan office.
Though tempted, I felt that the time had come to establish
a base of my own and wander no more.

Among those leading our work-group was a professor
from Oslo who had arrived cheerfully inebriated and
remained so throughout his stay. Because of a severe
alcohol shortage in Norway, the professor, picking up
bottles on his journey through Europe, had rolled onto
the platform in Venice and been carried to bed by the
welcoming committee. Feeling the need, perhaps, of a
steadying arm, he invited me to join him for dinner at the
home of Peggy Guggenheim. We travelled by gondola,
jumped onto the dark forecourt and groped towards the
lit windows beyond. On our way we collided with an
equestrian statue by Marino Marini. The rider's rampant
penis pointed towards Peggy Guggenheim's Palazzo. In

the dining room, the walls were crowded with paintings, many of them by her lovers. Ingrid Bergman, Rossellini and Henry Moore with his assuring North Country accent were among the guests. Little white dogs raced behind our short, stout hostess as she guided me to a toilet stuffed with the canvasses of Max Ernst, a lover perhaps in disgrace.

Compared with the small adventure of our arrival, the departure was an epic. Swaying stiffly, like a tree in the wind, the intoxicated professor had to be frog-marched towards the gondola by departing guests. My last glimpse of Peggy Guggenheim was of a small lady in white, shining in the dark, waving to us at the water's edge.

En route, our group was ejected at the nearest Fondamento by the irate gondolier. His curses echoed over the water long after he had disappeared into the night. The professor had vomited against the wind and soiled his black upholstery. We proceeded with difficulty over steps and bridges. Henry Moore manoeuvred the professor as though he was a wayward sheep on the Yorkshire moors, into the arms of the night-porter. Next morning, as we studied the adaptation of plate-glass to old buildings, he appeared again, cheerful and drunk.

It is sad for me to revisit the little Palazzo now that it has become the Guggenheim Museum and see the hostess, her ashes buried at the bottom of her garden, together with those of her little white dogs.

I had been in Venice for over a week now. Returning from a lecture on the perils inflicted on the city by vibrating motorboats (of which I had first-hand experience each night), I saw a shirt, socks and underwear hanging on a string across my room. A tall, dark man, naked but for his leather jacket, sat waiting for them to dry. Roberto Pozo, the long-awaited delegate from Havana, had arrived. The dripping clothes were most of his luggage. His black jacket had rotted in the creases, giving glimpses of Roberto's dark arms. The room was assuming, not inappropriately, the appearance of a refugee camp. Roberto was indeed a fugitive and a martyr to architectural theory.

He had graduated in Cuba and soon received his first commission, a country house for the American head of a gambling syndicate, an associate of Mafia boss Meyer Lansky. Plans were drawn up which the client approved before leaving on an extended stay in Miami. Work proceeded in the following months. It was then that Roberto saw Le Corbusier's latest book, expounding the novel theory that a man with his arm in the air represented the ideal height of a room. As a dutiful disciple he reduced all ceilings in the house to door height and continued building.

The American client returned, anxious to see the progress on his new country house. A motorcade drove to the site. What they saw from a distance, a large complex fit for pygmies, caused them to turn back to Havana without leaving their cars. The motorcade travelled in total and ominous silence. Before hit-men could arrive to convey the client's opinion on Corbusier's latest theory, Roberto's widowed mother had spirited her son out of their reach to Europe. For the moment at least the Venice Conference was his safe haven.

The laundry dried in time for us to walk to the Teatro Fenice. We had tickets for the gala performance of *Wozzeck*. Carabinieri with plumed hats guarded the grand staircase. We found our seats in what had been the Imperial box in times of Hapsburg splendour. The conductor of the orchestra had just arrived from abroad and when the opera was about to begin, he bowed deeply in the direction of the gold-encrusted Imperial box and the dark, leather-clad figure in the centre. There was no response. He bowed again, one arm pointing at the orchestra, the other raised towards Roberto in supplication. Every head in the crowded auditorium was turning towards the Imperial box and the mysterious ruler who sat there. Roberto, aware of his role at last, though reluctant to emerge from the shadows, rose, bowed graciously to the conductor and extended a cracked, leather sleeve towards the stage. The conductor raised his baton and the overture began.

I saw much of my roommate in the weeks ahead but, after Venice, we never met again. The Castro revolution came and the head of the gambling syndicate fled to Miami. Roberto was able to return to Cuba. I received an enthusiastic letter from him extolling the virtues of the new regime. Some years later, I saw him on the front page of an architectural magazine, which my cousin Fela sent me regularly from Poland. Stouter now and a little bald, he towered over a group of architects from the Eastern block, as he explained his model of a large, housing-project. 'Pozo: Architect of the Cuban Revolution', read one caption. I saw other projects of his in the magazine. His style seemed to be a synthesis of Socialist Realism and Caribbean chic and I wished him well.

Years passed and an attractive, dark lady came to my gallery in Jaffa, introducing herself as correspondent for Cuba's official newspaper *Gramma*. She brought regards for me from Roberto Pozo. 'How is the architect of the Cuban Revolution?' I asked. 'He has gone to Paris.' I enquired about his many projects at home. She replied that they had only been models and there had never been money to build any of them. Desperate to erect something in his lifetime, he had applied for leave to depart from Cuba. I asked how Fidel Castro had taken this. 'He was most understanding and even permitted Roberto to leave with fifty dollars.' I looked for a smile on the lady's face, but there was none. Times were hard for Roberto in Paris. Architects of the left-wing regarded him as a traitor to the revolution. To those on the right he was an unacceptable Communist. One day I saw that he had won the first prize for a conference centre in Yugoslavia. His plan was in the shape of a woman's torso. Her abdomen formed the major conference hall. The breasts were smaller assembly chambers. Entry appeared to be through the womb. The article that I read stressed the sense of well-being that would descend on an assembly gathered in a breast. But Tito, with his weakness for the torsos of ample women, died, and the project was never built. Since then I have lost touch with Roberto Pozo. I hope that he will return to Cuba after Castro and spearhead the next architectural revolution there. I await it with interest.

Jean-Paul Jeanneret, known as Le Corbusier (the raven), had arrived in Venice to lecture. He appeared in the auditorium, gaunt, grey, in a tweed jacket, wearing metal-rimmed glasses, like a stern accountant. The hall was overcrowded. I sat on the floor, next to Gérard Philippe who was in Venice to play Corneille's *El Cid* with the French National Theatre. On the stage, large sheets of paper had been suspended from an easel. With a thick crayon, Corbusier drew the sun, a quick sketch of the Doges' Palace and wavy lines, representing water. *'Venise!'* he said and stepped back. A group of acolytes hurried towards the paper and reverently placed it on the table. Next he drew a circle traversed by a wavy line. *'La coeur de la cité!'* he said and waited for the acolytes to remove it. The lecture proceeded with many quick sketches and profound clichés. I believe, in time, it became another of his books. I left, feeling that I had seen men turn into myth and myth turn into an industry. Somewhere, long ago, among a sea of adoring faces and outstretched hands, I had been immunised against adulation. It left me now with a slight sense of nausea.

I heard that Corbusier and his admirers had later marched towards a canal where he pointed at the oar-supports of a gondola and explained that their abstract beauty was a shape dictated by water and tide. That night, the gondoliers did brisk business selling their broken oar-supports. Next morning, I saw them cradled in the arms of Corbusier's followers as they strolled through Venice. Some days later, I thought myself more fortunate to hear a lecture on modern art by Bruno Zevi, an outstanding art historian from Rome. His wit and humanism made a welcome contrast to the cult of the Great Man.

'Will you come with me to Vicenza for the day?' asked Margot Racossy of the American delegation, in her charming blend of Bostonian with a Hungarian lilt. I looked into her blue eyes, at the fetching suntan, the short, flowered dress she wore and cancelled all other plans.

We had become friends after I retrieved her purse from the canal into which it fell, as she photographed the Arsenal bridge from a precarious angle. Her traveller's cheques safe and dry, she rewarded me with my first 'Bellini' at Harry's Bar, and took me to sit by the window at which, she claimed, Hemingway used to wait for the last rays of the sun to shine into the evening's first Martini.

We travelled to Vicenza by bus to see the Teatro Olimpico and Palladian villas. She photographed them at length, from all angles, material for a lecture on her return to Harvard. Margot's mother had been a ballerina in Hungary. I photographed her daughter now, pirouetting on the sloping stage of the theatre, among a scenery of false perspectives. A graceful shepherdess who had lost her

196

cardboard sheep. It was a hot evening when we sat in the market square waiting for the bus to return us to Venice. Nearby, a falcon chained to his perch, looked longingly at the pyramid of small, naked birds lying on a meat-stall.

Margot's parents had left Hungary, moved to Paris and were now in the United States. 'Where do you belong?' I asked and she replied, 'I am my own country.' After a pause, she added, 'and so are you.' It was probably true. But there was another question on my mind. 'What about Israel?' She poured the last of my coffee into a saucer and I assumed that Hungarian gypsies had taught her to read the future. But she only removed a drowning moth – for Israel she needed no coffee dregs. 'What a mess!' she said. 'Perhaps it will even be a country someday. A land full of neurotic Jews, all piled on top of each other.' She pointed at the plucked birds on the market stall. My question had not pleased her. As we walked to the bus, she took my hand. 'Why not come to Boston? They are building a lot and you could get your next degree at MIT.' 'Are you proposing a merger of our two countries?' I asked. 'A possible customs-union, in the course of time,' she replied, withdrawing her hand. In matters of diplomacy, Margot Racossy was clearly a more experienced country than I.

But thoughts of Israel remained and I wondered why they persisted. I was grateful to England, liked its people and culture, and if time had not made an Englishman of me, I had certainly become Anglicised. It seemed sensible to head for London, start my career in an architect's office and build up from there. That would be the advice of my relatives. The thoughts that troubled me, however, were not sensible.

My stay in Venice was nearing its end. I decided to combine a day of solitude with a visit to Ravenna. 'A long walk clears the mind and a cold shower clears the imagination,' our headmaster, the bishop, had often preached and I had taken his advice on the former, while avoiding the latter. In Ravenna, I walked through hot, dusty avenues flanked by cypress trees, entered the ancient churches and looked at their golden mosaics. Byzantine courtiers in ornamental robes looked down at me from walls and ceilings. Despite the haloes, they resembled a Levantine Mafia, their passions converted to tranquillity by the mosaic cubes that formed them. In this atmosphere, both peaceful and cool, I sat in a pew and returned to my preoccupations.

I could not forget that when the camps had opened after the war and survivors emerged, my parents had not been among them. Their absence left a void, an empty space, which to my mind was located in Israel. Had they lived, my father, as practical a man as any of the courtiers above me, no doubt would have headed for America. My mother's interest in a Jewish state probably amounted to a coin in the collection-box. But in death, they had been transformed into statistics of a terrible truth – the help-lessness of a people without a land. The new Jewish state, however modest and problematic its beginning, seemed a unique historic challenge and a symbol that gave meaning to the fate of my parents and millions like them. I owed it a visit, perhaps I owed it more. At the risk of annoying Margot Racossy, not to speak of my relatives in London, I came to a decision.

I took a last look at the Byzantine saints of San Vitale. 'Gentlemen, I am going east, in your direction. Any advice you can give . . .' They smiled back enigmatically.

Returning to Manchester, I stopped off at the Israeli Embassy in London. It was possible to arrange a working vacation in Israel through them. After some weeks they responded with a short list of proposals from architectural

offices. I chose one in Tel Aviv, where a university friend
had invited me to share his flat. My family in London were
also on the move. Elschen, my mother's younger sister,
had emigrated to Los Angeles. Ruth and Kurt were retir-
ing to Lausanne. Only my cousin Nils remained as an
intern at a hospital. In North London, my grandmother's
grave stood as a reminder of the family's stay in England.

During the weeks of waiting, I worked and prepared for
my departure, crated my books and bought what I
wrongly took to be the right clothes for a new climate. I
said goodbye to friends and took sentimental walks
through streets I did not expect to see again. I had become
a Mancunian of sorts, but not enough to suppose that I
would be dreaming about Manchester in faraway places.
And yet the spirits that hovered over the city and had
hurled the meteor into the university quadrangle, saw fit
to send me a parting present.

It came in the guise of a phone call. Before leaving for
Venice, I had met Hélène and George at a party. She was
a slim, attractive Belgian, in her mid-twenties. He, an
Alexandrian Greek, was dark, heavy and twice her age. As
I spoke with them about art, George had taken the ivory
pipe from his mouth long enough to invite me home for a
viewing of his Egyptian antiquities. It appeared to be a
sizeable collection, acquired at little expense from guards
at the Cairo Museum, who stole them to order. I suspected
that it might be the source of his livelihood and hoped that
he had not mistaken me for a prospective client.
Hypnotised by Hélène's shapely legs which rocked to and
fro before me as we spoke, I had agreed to show the university to George's sister on her coming visit to town.
Hélène's phone call now came to remind me of that
promise. I proposed the 'Friday Night Hop' at the
Students' Union as a suitable entrée into the university

and its amenities.

Large, dark eyes were sizing me up. George's sister, Mela, compact and brown like her brother, reminded me of a cat. A jet-black page-cut added to the illusion. Her English contained the melodies of Greek and French. Added to this, an upward glance with a click of the tongue meant 'no', while a finger pointing at the eye was an expression of serious doubt. 'No university hops in Alexandria,' she said as we danced, 'only private parties.' 'Are there clubs?' I asked. The tongue clicked. 'Forbidden. King Farouk goes. If he desires a woman, she must come.' She brought her lips close to my ear and wriggled her little finger 'His phallus,' she whispered solemnly, 'is half of this.' I felt that I was learning a great deal about Egypt. For Arabs she had only contempt. 'Greeks, Romans and Jews built Alexandria, then the Arabs came to ruin it.' Remembering that I too belonged to one of those categories, she shook her hands in the air as if to dry them. 'Greeks and Jews are like fire and water.' It sounded like a judgement transmitted through the mouths of her ancestors over the centuries. I had no need to ask which was which, remembering the waters Odysseus sailed and the Pillar of Fire in which God had appeared to the Hebrews.

But as the night progressed and the band changed its music from fast to slow, fire and water seemed to blend well. We walked home together after midnight. The autumn night was unseasonably warm and there was a park on our way. We made love on fallen leaves, sheltered by rhododendrons.

Over the weekend I wondered how many Alexandrian taboos I had broken, and at their consequences. It was a relief when Hélène called some days later with a dinner invitation. Mela was preparing a special Egyptian meal.

Hélène received me with a glass of wine and a kiss. Mela

was busy in the kitchen. I enquired about George. 'He is in Egypt on business.' A collection of pipes on the table were a reminder of him. I turned and faced a gold-clad, human figure with the head of a jackal. 'Anubis,' said Hélène as though making an introduction. 'Guardian of the Dead.' Next to him, men in white loin-cloths strained at the oars of a large wooden vessel. An assortment of scarab beetles lay in trays. Beyond an open door I saw two mummy cases. Hélène pointed to the smaller one. It contained an embalmed baboon. The larger one was empty. 'Do you want to get in?' Thinking it unlikely that I would lie in many mummy cases in the future, I removed my shoes and enclosed myself in an aroma of pitch and must. It felt warm and comfortable. 'I'll stay here for the night,' I said. 'There could be nicer ways to spend it,' was her reply and I wondered whether she had considered alternatives.

Mela called us to the dining room. I had expected other guests, but saw that the large choice of little dishes was intended only for three. We ate to Egyptian music. The plaintive voice of a woman rose above drums and strings. 'That's *Oum Kalsoum,*' explained Mela, translating the song. '*Anta Oumri* – You are my life.' We moved to the living room with our wine glasses and sat around a tray of Turkish delights and small coffee cups. Hélène and Mela lit cigarettes. I explained that I did not smoke, never having managed the trick of inhaling. The girls laughed. 'Open your mouth, we'll blow into you.' And so I inhaled the hashish fumes. Time passed in a pleasant and relaxing haze. Eventually the walls began to sway. Hélène, or perhaps Mela, was laughing and the jackal-headed Anubis suddenly looked down at me from the ceiling. Hélène, sitting on my lap, blew smoke into my mouth. The legs that had hypnotised me were now within reach, but my hands had a problem with their precise location. Moments of great clarity began to jostle with periods of oblivion. Hélène and Mela were kissing on an armchair, but how did we get upstairs to the bed in which we now lay? Mela and Hélène were with me on the bed, then I noticed them on the floor in a passionate embrace which seemed so odd that I had to laugh. Incense rose from red candles and the music had changed from Egyptian to Greek, '*Apopse philame*.' I watched in wonder as Greek monks, swinging censers, walked in procession out of the wallpaper and noticed that Anubis was one of them. Mela kissed me, her cat-like body on my chest and in her kisses was the scent of Hélène.

I awoke to the dawn chorus of birds, lying next to the girls, rose unsteadily and turned off the gramophone scratching on its last groove. The incense candles had burnt down, but the room was heavy with fumes. I made myself coffee, then returned to the bedroom to kiss Hélène and Mela who were still asleep. I left the house reluctantly, as if deserting a night that had given such great and unexpected pleasure. Towards my fellow conspirators I felt gratitude and love for the total physical joy they had planned and given.

Within days notice came that my job in Tel Aviv had been arranged and that I was expected. I spoke with Hélène and Mela on the phone, but we never met again. I wonder what other pleasures they devised before George returned with his new hoard of stolen antiquities? For months to come, at odd moments, the smell of hashish would suddenly assail me. Eventually it left me, but the warm memories of Mela and Hélène never will.

It seemed paradoxical that my embarkation for Israel would take me back to Venice once more. The city was flooded after heavy rain. The Piazza San Marco had been covered with planks which floated about in the current, as the tide continued to rise. People walked ankle-high in freezing water. The students, professors and artists who crowded the city a few weeks before had gone, and even the Venetians looked as though they would rather be elsewhere. Familiar places were empty. Café Florian was closed for repair.

I walked to the dryer part of town, to the market behind the Rialto Bridge. My friend in Tel Aviv had a fiancée and I wanted to buy her a silk scarf there. As I searched among the stalls, someone tapped me on the shoulder. 'Signore, were you once in Spain?' I turned and recognised the travel companion with whom I had crossed the Pyrenees at Port Bou, six years before. 'I thought that you lived in Spain,' I said, 'What are you doing here?' '*Ah signore, gli Spagnoli sono dei maleducati*, not hospitable like the Italians and also, the country is very poor.' I remembered his name – Franco. He had married, his wife was expecting a baby and the market stall belonged to her. He left it in the care of a neighbour while we walked to a bar. 'Do you remember the Civil Guards, those bastards who stole my coffee and cigarettes? Of course, they did not find the most important thing!' I asked what they had overlooked. He smiled, patted his stomach and I was afraid to inquire further.

Invited to join Franco at home for dinner, I returned to the market stall in the evening and we walked to his flat on the Campo San Jacobo. His wife greeted us with a fine meal, after which we sat back to finish the Chianti I had purchased for the occasion. Once the baby arrived, they intended to move to the mainland and live in Mestre. 'It's growing fast, they've got industry there and I'm a good motor mechanic.' He pointed to a picture on the wall, Franco in uniform. His chin was thrust forward and there was a garlanded slogan above his head; '*Credere, Combattere, Obbedire!*' 'I was Brigadiere in a motorcycle unit until the English captured us. As a prisoner, I made more money repairing boots for British officers than I did as a Brigadiere. But that's all in the past now, signore, the uniform, the black-shirt. New times for Italy and for him,' he pointed to his wife's stomach. 'I vote Communist these days, the party of the Working Man.'

I asked where he came from. 'Padua, up the Brenta canal. We're a hard people there. An angel once came to a man in Padua and told him to make a wish. "Anything?" asked the Padovano. "Yes," said the angel. "What's the catch?" "No catch," said the angel, "but whatever you wish for, your neighbour will get double." The Padovano thought about it, then turned to the angel and said, "Take out one of my eyes." But for all that, I learned that a man should stay close to his home and not travel too much. Perhaps you also travel too much, signore, Spain, England, Italy, now Israel. You should stay close to your home.' 'I had a home once,' I said. 'It met with a historical accident and now it's gone.' He nodded, '*L' ebreo vagante.*' (The wandering Jew.) Though I did not like the analogy, it contained a certain truth.

Hearing that I was to embark the following afternoon he insisted on taking me to the ship. 'A man must have a friend to see him off and a friend to meet him.' And so, the next day, Franco and I dragged a heavy suitcase from the Pensione to the ship. On the way I realised that my suitcase was blue, like the one Fimek and my father had bought me in Warsaw, when my journey began.

The ship was anchored next to the Doggana, the imposing customs house on which two giants struggle to balance a golden sphere. There, Franco and I parted. I stored my case in the cabin, went up on deck and leaned over the rusty railings. Venice looked grey and forlorn. For centuries, pilgrims had sailed from this place bound for the 'Holy Land'. Their recorded complaints about watered wine, insolent galley slaves and corrupt captains, crowded the vaults of the Doge's palace. Watching a ship's officer eat a live fish and a sailor beat a colleague unconscious with a chair, I was certain that this crew would be a credit to their ancestors.

Laughter, music and enraged shouting now came from the lower deck. The purser, hysterical in his fury, was tearing at his white uniform. A group of Brazilian late-comers had lost their collective passports. '*Imbecilli! Ubriachi! Mi state uccidendo!*' he screamed, while the Brazilians sang and danced around him, one playing a flute, another a small drum which manipulated from inside, produced the squealing of a pig. I had heard my first samba.

The freight and passengers finally aboard, the gangplanks were raised. The engines vibrated, the ship shuddered and from the vent-shafts of the galley came the smell of a meal I preferred to miss. It was raining again. The ship raised anchor and steamed off into a rough sea, towards Brindisi and the East. Flying behind us, a convoy of gulls waited for the crew to dump the first pile of garbage into the sea. Venice soon disappeared in a cloak of fog.

I did not harbour the illusion that I was going home, but rather the expectation that I might build one.

Postscript

A PUBLIC SCULPTURE of mine was recently unveiled in Spain, in the town of Gerona. Two years had passed since I attended a similar occasion in Miami and began this book.

I remembered Gerona as a railway stop on the way from Port Bou, where I crossed the French border to visit my uncle Kurt, in Barcelona in 1947. On the day of the inauguration, I drove again to Port Bou and the border crossing in the Pyrenees. An efficient new customs house stands there now, with barriers controlling the flow of traffic from France. A blue plaque displays the gold stars of the European Community. A short distance away, I found the remains of the bunker where my Italian travelling companion and I were examined by Civil Guards those many decades ago. Only the bunker's cracked concrete roof remains as a support for the rocks above.

Driving back to Port Bou, I saw, as I had done on that first time, the Mediterranean and the little town on the shore. The serpentine road had been widened. In Port Bou, the short 'Rambla' where the fiesta had been held in 1947 appeared unchanged. A small promenade now separates the last houses from the rough beach through which I waded then. At waterfront cafés, French tourists were enjoying their first drinks in Spain.

Enclosed by whitewashed walls, a cemetery is perched

on a cliff above. Next to it, a memorial was recently erected
to the German philosopher and critic, Walter Benjamin,
commemorating the fiftieth year of his suicide at Port Bou.
It recalls also the inhumanity of the Civil Guards of the
town, who threatened to hand him back to the Germans
and drove him to take his own life. It was designed by a
friend of mine from Tel Aviv, who also created a park in
the old ramparts of Jaffa, where I live. The memorial is a
rectangular, metal conduit, which descends diagonally
through the rocks and emerges at a cliff above the sea. One
walks through the tunnel, down metal steps, towards a
plate-glass wall, which acts as a barrier between the visitor
and the turbulent waters. Below, the sea hurls foam onto the
sharp rocks. A quotation from Walter Benjamin has been
sand-blasted into the glass: 'It is more arduous to honour the
memory of the nameless, than that of the renowned. History
is devoted to the memory of the nameless.'

Standing at that glass wall, I felt that I had come full
circle, out of the past and back again to where it began. Let
Walter Benjamin's sentence stand as the epitaph for my
parents, relatives, friends and all those I encountered,
who, with no glass wall to protect them, were hurled down
onto sharp rocks.

Miami 1992–Gerona 1994

Epilogue

THE PLANE FROM TEL AVIV will reach Moscow some hours after midnight. I will unpack in the light of dawn and take my place, a little later, at a conference table with officials from Moscow's City Hall. A memorial shrine is to be built in the capital, commemorating 200,000 Jewish soldiers of the Red Army who fell in the war against Hitler's Germany. The work must be completed by Victory Day, May 1997.

I look beyond these next intensive days, to the moment when I sit in a fish and chip shop in north London with my friend David Goldberg. We have met there over the years to exchange news, talk politics and gossip a little. Once, in an Italian church, I saw a Gothic fresco of Hell and noticed that amongst the shadows cast by writhing sinners and busy devils, two men were painted engrossed in amiable conversation. For me that is 'time out' for fish and chips with David.

We first met over two decades ago. He was a newly ordained rabbi, I was about to switch from being an architect, whose hobby was sculpting, to a sculptor whose hobby would not be architecture. (For my wife's encouragement to take that leap I will be ever appreciative.)

Meanwhile David has become the senior rabbi of a major London synagogue. He continues to write and was fiercely active in promoting the Arab-Israeli dialogue, acceptable now but controversial when he first fought for it. We debated that and much else. I often filled up the napkins of our meals with biblical passages he suggested for the projects I had been commissioned to undertake. In time they have appeared cast in metal and stone in Florida, Germany and Buenos Aires.

When I felt that the time had come to write about Danzig, the city I came from, now long destroyed, and the people who lived there, long dead, it seemed natural to approach David with my first pages. As he tentatively fingered them, I saw a bubble form in the air just above his head and read the words 'My God! Now he thinks he can write!'

At the time David was completing a book of his own and was about to retreat into the country to work. My manuscript accompanied him also. Some weeks later we met again. 'Well, Frank,' he said, 'Michelangelo you may be – Dante you're not!' But fortunately David also said, 'I like what you've written, write lots more and I'll help you.'

I wrote more and sent it in relays to David. I became accustomed to seeing my favourite passages firmly crossed out, question marks in the margins, footnotes like 'Supply more detail' or 'You can do better than that!'

Time progressed and pages gathered. A day came when David introduced me to his literary agent, Vivienne Schuster, and over a few enjoyable margaritas I distinctly heard her say that the manuscript had potential. Together, we decided the direction it should take.

In the two years that have passed, David's comments and seminars on sequence and style have coaxed the book into shape. It also found a publisher. As midwife or (given his vocation) Godfather of this book, I hope David is moderately pleased with the sprog that was born. I am hugely grateful to him.

I hope that we will meet many more times in our fish and chip shop, and just for now, 'How about a bit of cod-roe and haddock?'

Bibliography

Jan Bakker, *Pommern*, Gerhard Rautenberg, 1988.

Carl J. Burckhardt, *Meine Danziger Mission*, Deutscher Taschenbuch Verlag, 1962.

S. Echt, *Die Geschichte der Juden in Danzig*, Rautenberg, 1972.

Jan Kilarski, *Gdansk*, Maritime and Colonial League, Warsaw, 1937.

B. Leverton, S. Lovenson, *I Came Alone: The Stories of the Kindertransports*, Book Guild, 1990.

H. S. Levine, *Hitler's Free City*, Chicago, 1973.

Hans Lewald, *Danzig so wie es war*, Droste, 1974.

Erwin Lichtenstein, *Die Juden der freien Stadt Danzig unter der Herrschaft des Nationalsozialismus*, G. C. B. Mohr, Paul Siebeck, 1973.

Carl Tighe, *Danzig: National Identity in the Polish–German Borderlands*, Pluto, 1990.

Danzig 1939: Treasures of a Destroyed Community, The Jewish Museum, New York.

Documents Concerning German–Polish Relations and the Outbreak of Hostilities Between Great Britain and Germany on September 3, 1939, HMSO, London, 1939.